g. N. Luciani

Please visit my website at:
www.georgenluciani.com

"I have known and worked with George for over twenty years. He is the consummate professional in managing his clients' money."
—Robert H. McLaren, CPA
McLaren & Co., P.C.

"Having known George Luciani for over twenty-five years professionally, I was impressed from the beginning with his leadership in the financial-planning profession, his early adoption of the financial-planning process as central to clients meeting their goals, and his quest for excellence that led him to find a way to minimize conflicts of interest. His ability to communicate life experiences that resonate with clients and to provide solutions to fit their lifestyles today, adjusting to changing events as necessary, provides the roadmap. But getting to the end goal requires a guide, one with investment acumen adept at evaluating the changing opportunities and their implications in different economic times. George has been that guide for years, and this book makes the way clear."
—Constance J. Herrstrom, MBA, CFP®
president/owner, Premier Financial Planning, Inc.

"Many books are written about financial planning, but few connect with everyday people. This book certainly hits the mark by making you understand the connection between using sound financial advice to achieve your life's goals. This is possible with a proper attitude, a plan, and of course, the right advisor! I have known George for over eighteen years, and he has always been true to his above-reproach advisory style. The book provides common sense, straightforward financial-planning advice for those who will listen. Keeping the cherries and throwing away the pits is a great metaphor for life, managing your money, and the pursuit of happiness!"
—Christopher "Chris" Nardo
president/CEO, Monument Bank, Doylestown, PA

KEEP THE
CHERRIES
THROW AWAY THE PITS

KEEP THE
CHERRIES
THROW AWAY THE PITS

DOES YOUR FINANCIAL ADVISOR
KNOW THE DIFFERENCE?

GEORGE N. LUCIANI, CFP®

Advantage®

Published by Advantage, Charleston, South Carolina.
Member of Advantage Media Group.

ADVANTAGE is a registered trademark, and the Advantage colophon is a trademark of Advantage Media Group, Inc.

Printed in the United States of America.

ISBN: 978-1-59932-727-3
LCCN: 2016938009

Book design by George Stevens.

Author photo by Frank Pronesti of Heirloom Studio.

This publication is designed to provide accurate and authoritative information in regard to the subject matter covered. It is sold with the understanding that the publisher is not engaged in rendering legal, accounting, or other professional services. If legal advice or other expert assistance is required, the services of a competent professional person should be sought.

Advantage Media Group is proud to be a part of the Tree Neutral® program. Tree Neutral offsets the number of trees consumed in the production and printing of this book by taking proactive steps such as planting trees in direct proportion to the number of trees used to print books. To learn more about Tree Neutral, please visit **www.treeneutral.com.** To learn more about Advantage's commitment to being a responsible steward of the environment, please visit **www.advantagefamily.com/green**

Advantage Media Group is a publisher of business, self-improvement, and professional development books and online learning. We help entrepreneurs, business leaders, and professionals share their Stories, Passion, and Knowledge to help others Learn & Grow. Do you have a manuscript or book idea that you would like us to consider for publishing? Please visit **advantagefamily.com** or call **1.866.775.1696.**

*Considering that Cherries is a compendium of my professional life, I
would be remiss not to dedicate this work to the people in my family
for their encouragement in writing it. In particular, my two sons, Marc
and Matthew, both of whom have chosen careers in finance.*

*The philosophy behind this book, however, comes from my formative
years, growing up with my brother, Bob; my sister, Evelyn; and of
course my parents, Umberto and Elizabeth, now deceased. My father
came to America as a child from a small town on the Adriatic shores
of Abruzzo. My mother was the first child of her family to be born
in America. In spite of their limited educational opportunities, both
understood the value of higher education for their children. Dad was
a welder but also sang opera with the Philadelphia Opera chorus for
fifteen years. Mom was a seamstress and also sang in the choir of our
local church. Both instilled in us the value of work and the undying
love of family. I am proud to be their son.*

ACKNOWLEDGMENTS

Many people and institutions have been an influence on my professional life that supports the information contained in this book including the Financial Planning Association (FPA), formerly the Institute of Certified Financial Planners (ICFP), where the concept of financial planning originated in the early 1970s. We crafted a profession that today is recognized worldwide.

My growth as a professional was also aided by the many accountants and attorneys I have and do work with on behalf of client interests. With over seventy-seven thousand pages in the US tax code, no one individual knows it all. Collaborating with other professionals is critical in executing a client's financial plan.

I also have to thank my clients for their continued trust in my judgment and their diligence and sometimes useful and constructive criticism over these many years of service.

I would also be remiss if I did not acknowledge my other family, Burdette Russo and Kylie Keegan, whose artful eyes and judgement helped me decide on the proper cover design for this book.

Many thanks to my staff, past and present, particularly Dorie McCarthy who has edited my monthly client commentaries for many years; Annie Stiles, CFP® who helped proof the technical data;

and my personal assistant, Caren Habermehl, whose diligent work with clients and patience with me cannot be overstated.

A great deal of thanks to my business associates and friends, Connie Herrstrom, CFP®; Bob McLaren, CPA; Frank Sullivan, JD; and Chris Nardo for their kind testimonial thoughts.

A great deal of thanks and appreciation must be offered to my lifelong friend, Bob DiRomualdo, who wrote the foreword for this manuscript. As young teenagers, Bob and I had adjoining newspaper routes in West Philadelphia where we both grew up of humble beginnings. We both earned money for college through our own diligence and perseverance. Bob also was a Navy airman during Vietnam, came home to earn an MBA at Harvard, and later became president and CEO of Borders before retiring at the height of the bookstore explosion he started. Bob is one of the great visionaries of our time.

Finally, to Bob Sheasley, my book editor whose excellent wordsmithing helped to chisel a ninety-thousand word exercise down to this refined work. Great job Bob.

TABLE OF CONTENTS

FOREWORD

Financial planning is a very serious business. A high-quality CFP® (Certified Financial Planner™) has an important seat at the family table. He (or she) can be the difference between a comfortable retirement or years of stress and angst. The job changes throughout the life cycle, starting with convincing the young (and immortal) to begin planning for retirement. As life goes on and the family's earnings capacity emerges, risk tolerances are fine-tuned. The CFP® must opine on the appropriate use of insurance at the various stages of life. The proper use of credit is a huge factor as well. In short, the CFP® starts off conducting a small combo, but as the family moves through life amassing the complexities that come with building a family, and the enormous expense of higher education emerges, he is conducting a full symphony, often with choral accompaniment. In most cases, the aim is to plan for a lifestyle in retirement that is reasonably consistent with the years leading up to that day. Having this occur is no small task.

The CFP® must counter the "live for today" attitudes of the young and the use of credit to attain instant gratification, as well as the fifty-something's desire to add risk in an unwise fashion. When the press is hyping the bubble of the day, be it dot-com, housing, credit, gold, or whatever, the CFP® must bring the client back into the real world. Most importantly, the CFP® must make clients understand that with increasing life expectancy, many will live nearly as long in retirement as years actually worked—and the mathematical facts of life that come with it. The sad fact is that most folks don't have such a person on their team. Unfortunately, they suffer the consequences for many years. I have seen this all too often firsthand.

George Luciani has written a book that explains this long, complex road in everyday language that can be enjoyed by workers of all ages. I first met George when he took over his brother's paper route more than fifty years ago. I have seen his career develop via roads that led in many directions. That is until, while selling financial products, he had the light bulb go off and realized that he wasn't really solving his clients' problems. He took to real financial planning like a duck to water and, for so many years, has been the maestro who has bettered the lives of so many families. To say that he takes his role seriously is an understatement. He has had clients walk rather than agree to investments that simply made no sense for their particular circumstances, no matter what the market hype of the day. Sure, he has earned a nice living. But in addition, he has that added bonus of seeing so many enjoy their golden years. Now, with the writing of *Keep the Cherries, Throw Away the Pits,* George is passing on decades of hard-earned wisdom in a highly readable book that will help working people and families of all ages and income levels. It is a chance for many to start down the road to a better future.

—*Robert DiRomualdo, founder and CEO, Naples Ventures, LLC*

PREFACE

KEEP THE CHERRIES,
THROW AWAY THE PITS

Cherries is a different narrative on the financial-services industry. The impetus for this work comes from my desire to inform the average investor about the sales practices that surround the financial-advisory practices, many of which may be hazardous to your financial health. I have witnessed these conditions for more than thirty years, first as a broker and then as a Registered Investment Advisor (RIA). In this book, I have provided some information that might be useful in separating the salespeople from the true advisors.

In reading through this book, you may be surprised to learn how few standards exist to separate those who call themselves "financial advisors" from those who are credentialed in some form of professional manner. Most people know that a CPA is a certified public accountant. But how many people know or understand the training and testing required for becoming and maintaining the Certified Financial Planner™ (CFP®) designation?

Does a broker who passes a securities test know how to manage an investment portfolio that has taken you years to develop? Given uncertain market conditions, are they truly trained to know which securities they should keep (cherries) and which to sell (pits)?

Medical doctors and lawyers are *fiduciaries* to their clients, which means they must put the client's best interest above their own. Which financial advisors also have this legal fiduciary responsibility to their clients? Why have the large brokerage houses resisted having the Securities and Exchange Commission (SEC) put the "fiduciary" tag on their broker salespeople?

Do insurance people who market annuities to retired seniors use deceptive sales practices to lure the uninformed into products that are complicated in structure, are expensive to maintain, and provide high commissions to the brokers? How is it possible for any financial product to offer high returns with no risk? If you believe there is a free lunch, you also believe in the tooth fairy.

Most importantly, *why* is it important for even the average person to do a financial plan with a qualified CFP®? With many people living longer lives, how can the financial issues of an extended lifespan play out once the working-income years are over? Qualified professionals (cherries) are mixed in the financial marketplace with the not-so-qualified salespeople (pits). The wrong choice can definitely leave a bad taste in your mouth (and your life savings).

One of the most profound quotes I have ever heard was at a conference many years ago. I apologize to the speaker whose name escapes me. It rings true with the purpose of this book: "Where you will be five years from today will depend upon two things: the books that you read and the people with whom you associate."

The rest is in your hands.

—George N. Luciani

INTRODUCTION

SO MUCH MORE THAN MONEY

When I was a rookie advisor in the 1980s, newly licensed to sell insurance and securities, I found myself one morning in a New York City training room ready to learn the ropes. My fellow trainees and I were each given a Manhattan phone book and escorted to a chair next to a telephone.

"Pick a page, any page," our trainer told us, "and start dialing." Our mission was to sell a $10,000 corporate bond, and we were given a sheet describing it. The focus in those days was on straight commissions. The goal was to get a check and open an account. This was about making the sale—not about developing a relationship or putting the client's best interest first.

"Don't put that phone down!" the trainer called out to us as we set to work. "Keep going, right on down the page. Don't stop. If they're not interested, dial the next one." As we wore out our fingers, the trainer paced about the room. And every fifteen minutes or so, he shouted out this phrase:

"Keep the cherries, throw away the pits!"

As we sat through hours of that, we got the message: if they were interested, keep them on the line. If they were not, then they were

1

the pits. Move on to the next name in the phone book. Move on to the next possibility for success.

In the years since, much has changed in my career and in the industry. I think often of that trainer's exhortation, and over the decades, the meaning of his words has morphed. Though that was a lesson in sales, in a way it was also a metaphor for so many things in life.

If something is not going well, should you just keep repeating it in hopes that it will? How long do you pursue an idea that doesn't seem to be working? At what point does persistence become obstinance? When do you recognize a mistake and throw away those pits? Or better still—avoid the pits before a mistake is made?

In my financial-planning career, I have seen how the cherry-pit principle applies to investments. When they are going up, it is easy to hold on to them. It's not so easy when they are going down, although some investors cling to them presuming a rebound is just around the corner. They don't seem to see that the bottom could be zero, which means the company is out of business. As we all have observed, it sometimes happens.

The best traders and advisors are adept at knowing when to cut losses and move on to something else. They don't hold on to the losers. They know the difference between the cherries and the pits. Unfortunately, there are plenty who do not know the difference. They have no process and no idea when they should let go. Most people who call themselves financial advisors are simply salespeople.

There's no such thing as perfection in investing or in life. Quite often, as in horseshoes, being close is almost as good as being exact. If money is invested well 80 percent of the time, those good investments will result in significant gains. Competent advisors are skilled at analyzing an individual's financials and then determining which investment options are most likely to accomplish their goals.

CHANGING THE INDUSTRY

I was thirty-eight years old that day in the New York City training room. I had been a corporate executive for sixteen years, with managerial and sales experience that suited me well for a new career. In 1984, there were no such things as fiduciary advisors who operated on a fee-only basis. Registered Investment Advisors were not part of the industry. Those who entered the business back then were commission-based salespeople. They made money by selling, and if they didn't sell anything, they didn't eat.

I soon recognized that this was not how I wanted to work. This was not my vision for how people should be treated. In 1986, two years after I started, I discovered the Certified Financial Planner™ (CFP®) designation, which at the time was little known. Nobody knew what it meant. I had been selling insurance on a transaction basis, convinced that my education and knowledge could take me far beyond that. I became intrigued at the prospect of becoming a CFP® licensee.

At the time, there were two similar designations: CFP® and ChFC®, or Chartered Financial Consultant®. Since the latter was an insurance-industry designation and I had been selling insurance at an agency in Cranford, New Jersey, it might have seemed sensible for me to go that route. However, I chose the three-letter one that I figured might remind folks of "CPA." Sometimes the simplest logic works best.

And so I studied hard, even as I was working twelve-hour days in sales to feed my young family. It took two years of studying and six separate tests to earn the CFP® designation. To keep the designation requires thirty additional hours of study every two years, as well as a course every two years in ethics—a major emphasis. I was on track to a fulfilling career, and it turned out that I had made a good choice: today, seventy-three thousand people in this country carry the CFP® designation (CFP Board of Standards 2016).

When I started Capital Planning Advisory Group in 1988, I began offering asset management for a fee. This was a new phenomenon in the fields of financial planning and investments. I charged $500 for the first plan I did, even though it took more than twenty hours to create. I had no idea what to charge, so I just made up a price. This idea was so new that there was not yet a model or structure. Meanwhile, for several years I was still selling insurance for commission—because my family had to eat. Insurance sales are lucrative. Commissions can be 50 to 70 percent of the first year's premium.

By 1996, I had developed a substantial group of clients who were paying me fees on their investments. It was sufficient-enough recurring income to allow me to stop selling insurance. We went fee-only that year, which even then was unusual for planning and investments. Later in the nineties though, the CFP® designation rapidly grew. We were taking many clients away from the major broker-dealers, the ones that are household names. They were losing a fortune—and so, after years of disparaging the fee model, they too started to charge fees for investment advice rather than commissions.

We changed the industry. Today, most high-net-worth people invest on a fee-only basis because the advice comes without conflict of interest. For occasional investors of relatively small sums, nothing is wrong with paying a commission. Affluent investors, however, often consider commissions to be inappropriate. If you're selling Ford stock and buying General Motors stock and someone makes a commission on both ends, you are left to wonder whether it's just churn, an illegal activity that involves needlessly replacing one security for another. Commission brokers can easily make 1 to 3 percent a year in the buying and selling. Investors generally have no idea how much they are paying.

BEYOND THE INVESTMENTS

If a financial plan were a car, the investments would be the gasoline that makes it go. The finest automobile will just sit in the driveway without that fuel. Likewise, the fanciest financial plan is meaningless without money to execute it.

Money matters. The only people who can afford to say they don't care about money are those who have plenty of it. It is the fuel to get to the destination. It allows people to do what they find worthwhile in life. It fills their tank so that they can get going.

Some people truly desire to be charitable with their money. That is part of their plan. They want to give back to the community. Others want to build a legacy for their families so that they and their heirs can comfortably live the good life. Many wish to do both, to varying degrees at different times of life. A financial plan should be flexible, a work in progress. It must be suited to the individual.

The big financial houses do not really support financial planning of that nature. They have come to understand that it is important to high-net-worth people, and so they have representatives on staff who can take down a lot of information and put something together, bound in leather—and then they are done. For the most part, they are on to the next case. They provide a financial plan to help the broker get the account. The plan amounts to a *door opener*.

A true financial plan is not meant to be set up on a shelf. It should be based on a family relationship with an advisor that continues over the years, and it should be revised annually. I recently revised a plan for a corporate executive with whom I have worked for thirty years. She is now retiring at sixty. We are working out the cash flow from her investments to provide an income to age ninety and beyond. She is in a position to do that because of all those years that we have been working together, planning and adjusting the course along the way.

An airplane doesn't fly in a straight line. The navigator constantly adjusts for wind and climate conditions and for the most efficient flight path. The crew monitors all the variables. I have a client who is a glider pilot. He can fly from Pennsylvania to West Virginia and back without landing. "You just have to know how to read the thermals and the air currents," he told me. I understand, in my own way. Designing a financial plan requires that kind of finesse. Keeping the destination in mind, I look for the currents and adjust accordingly.

So much of this is learned behavior. He doesn't just ride those thermals by instinct, like a hawk. Daniel Kahneman, professor emeritus at Princeton University and a Nobel laureate in economics, developed the concept of *behavioral finance*. His book *Thinking Fast and Slow* is a seminal work on the subject. It refers to what psychologists call "system one" and "system two" of the human mind, which are our instinctive and learned behaviors. Through experience, we gain perceptions and perspective. We come to understand things because we have seen them before. That's the value in an experienced doctor, for example. And that's the value in an experienced financial advisor, who goes beyond the investments to understand the people who are making those choices.

Some say history doesn't repeat itself, but it certainly has patterns. It is through experience and training that those patterns become clear. That is how we learn to drive a car or gain any skill. That is how we advance in a career. There are patterns, too, in our behavior. That is why the themes of history, if not the specific events, are repetitive. And that is why people make the same mistakes, over and over, in their investments. They get greedy. They succumb to fear. Those characteristics are part of human nature, and we need to be aware of them before we can overcome them.

GETTING THROUGH THE STORMS

Sometimes investors need a third party with experience and training to save them from themselves. When the market is plummeting and people start panicking, someone with a cool head has to respond, "I know how to get us through this." Someone who understands the patterns and currents needs to be steadfast at the helm, like a captain steering a ship through a squall. He knows from experience just what to do so the ship won't capsize.

Such a role requires skill and stamina—and extensive training. My life partner, Burdette, swims thirty laps three times a week, but I guarantee that she won't be jumping out of a helicopter in a storm to save a life. She understands that she lacks the training. She wouldn't know all the right maneuvers that a professional rescue team would employ.

Experienced advisors know how to make it through financial storms, such as those in 2000 and 2008. They can't singlehandedly tame the choppy seas, but they have the knowledge and training to make the best decisions. They know the maneuvers, and they take action. They don't just sit back and say, "This will pass, don't worry about it." People perish that way.

That sort of guidance requires cultivating a relationship based on trust. Not just anyone can dispense wisdom. You will be far more likely to listen to someone who knows you and your family well and who understands your objectives in life and your deepest concerns.

No matter how much money they have, people nearing retirement seem to share a fundamental concern: Will they have enough? Will their savings and investments be enough to see them through for the rest of their lives while maintaining their accustomed lifestyle? Will they be able to preserve what they have put together and perhaps have plenty left over for their heirs? Running out of money is like running out of breath. Neither has a desirable outcome.

In essence, people's number-one fear is that their wealth is insufficient—and in the world of investment, fear and greed are the two prime emotional motivators. People tend to fear when they feel they lack control. They may tremble in an airplane but gleefully speed down a superhighway, even though they are far more likely to die in a car crash. In the driver's seat, though, they feel in control. In a plane, someone else is in control. They might presume the pilot is competent, but they don't know that person. There is no relationship.

In the world of money, people likewise sense that lack of control in many ways. They cannot control the economy or the stock market. They cannot control inflation. They cannot control geopolitical risk. They cannot issue orders to the Federal Reserve Bank. And therefore, as the market does its acrobatics, they succumb to fear or greed and try to make the most of whatever control they can muster. They still don't know the pilot, however. They often lack the relationship that could bring them safely down to earth.

Often people do not know whether they have enough, because they don't really know how much they have. That's why they need help. Whether the money will be sufficient depends on a variety of variables, including longevity. Nobody knows when they will die, so how can they know for sure whether they have enough for a lifetime? It's another of the many uncertainties that breeds the fear that leads to bad decisions.

Psychologists report that women, for many reasons, tend to be more concerned than men about running out of money. That does not mean that women are less competent or less aggressive investors. Certainly I have seen, in my years of working with couples, that women tend to be in charge of the household finances, and they are good stewards. To me, the difference means only that both partners should participate in the financial-planning process. Advisors need to hear their individual perspectives in order to draft the best plan for both. It is often the woman who ends up the survivor of a marriage and thus is confronted with long-term-care issues.

There is much you can do to dispel fear and gain reassurance that you will do just fine in retirement—and it starts with getting a grip on yourself. Namely, what are your resources, and what do you intend to do with them? You need to start early, develop a relationship with the right advisor, and build a plan for prosperity. That is how you regain control.

KNOWING THE RIGHT QUESTIONS

Most people lack the time to give their investments the kind of oversight that is essential to success. They cannot keep a daily eye on what is going on, which is why many people delegate that responsibility. A good advisor will provide the necessary oversight. That does not at all mean that he or she will make daily changes to the portfolio. The advisor should watch for trends, keep track of the positions, and monitor how well they are doing compared to the market. By keeping a close watch, the advisor will be able to raise yellow flags and perhaps red flags that require timely execution. This requires a level of vigilance that investors with busy lives realize they cannot sustain.

Frankly, many people understand that they lack the expertise to raise those flags themselves. They lack the perspectives that come from experience with the market and from years of regularly monitoring the behavior of investments. A good advisor knows "money knows no holiday." Missing a beat can mean losing an opportunity or suffering a penalty, regardless of the calendar.

When I meet with clients, however, we talk about much more than investments and portfolio performance. Mostly we talk about things that seemingly have little to do with their investments but that have everything to do with where they are going in life. We chat about their children and grandchildren, health issues, vacation plans, and more. We talk about life—and because that's really what money is all about, it is all germane. Good advisors listen intently, identify issues, and then apply their knowledge to find solutions. To come up with answers, one must first know the questions.

CHANGING PERSPECTIVES

When I worked in the insurance industry in the 1980s, the underwriters spoke of the "rule of self-exception," which basically is the attitude that "the other guy will get sick and die, but not me." Younger people by their nature tend to feel that way—some don't even bother with health insurance—but at some point, they start to wise up. They start to see a few of their friends and relatives pass away . . . and from health issues, not from accidents. Insurance actuaries for years considered age thirty-nine to be the crossover age at which health issues became the more common cause of death. That crossover age no doubt is a bit older now, but in any case, people clearly get a different perspective on their mortality as they age.

When they get into their forties, their financial perspectives also begin to change, and they think about preparing for retirement;

although, in the last thirty years, as life expectancy continues to increase, I have observed that people are waiting longer to properly plan. Today it seems that many are closer to age fifty before they start considering themselves to be at the halfway point.

Retirement is certainly on the minds of most of my clients. Two clients, both women and both educated and mentally sharp, were centenarians before they passed away. One gentleman, a World War II veteran who was wounded in the South Pacific, is ninety-five now. He and his wife both were skiing into their late eighties. He has been a client for twenty-five years, and their children, who are in their sixties and seventies, are clients as well.

Most of those with whom I work, though not all, have a net worth of over $1 million, including the value of their homes, and they are in the higher tax brackets. They are the type who are often called "the millionaires next door." They have attained affluence, but they seem like regular folks. One longtime client who is a multimillionaire drives a modest car with a manual transmission. "Why don't you get a Mercedes or BMW?" I asked him once at lunch. "No way," he said. "You can't get those with a stick shift."

Many of my clients are corporate executives, and I have seen them advance in their careers over the years. Today, as they approach retirement, they might have millions of dollars in their retirement and personal accounts. In my own executive career before going into financial services, I worked for Xerox, Basic American Foods, and Keebler. I understand the issues that executives face in their finances, such as how to deal with stock options. I have clients with Johnson & Johnson, AT&T—many of the big firms, and a lot of smaller ones as well.

Those who are nearing retirement have generally begun to think more conservatively about their investments, although often they refer us to their children who are still in the more aggressive accumulation stage. They do not tend to live an ostentatious lifestyle. In fact, some maintain a frugality that no doubt contributed to their ability to gain such wealth. They are not what you might call high-maintenance people.

Most people who are nearing retirement are concerned about preservation of capital, although they run the gamut in their lifestyle expectations. Multimillionaires certainly are not all the same. I have some clients of that net worth who need only $50,000 a year for living expenses. Others need $200,000 a year to make ends meet.

That's up to them. My job is not to preach to anyone about how much they should spend. My job is to help them continue their desired lifestyle without breaking stride when the paychecks stop. We replace that paycheck with other streams of income so that they can continue the status quo, whatever it might be. They should be able to drive the same kind of vehicles, take just as many vacations, and dine out wherever and whenever they desire.

There comes a time, of course, when people slow down. Not everyone will be skiing at ninety. Young people might imagine themselves enjoying retirement someday with the same supple thirty-year-old body that they have at present. Unfortunately, it doesn't turn out that way. The ski trips and the golf outings eventually become fewer, replaced with other joys. Some expenses diminish during retirement, while others grow.

Life changes, perspectives change, and priorities change—and a good financial planner will help to adjust the course. Salesperson advisors won't be able to help with those matters. It's not that they don't care, but it is not their focus. Life within a broker-dealer workplace is driven by sales targets that don't allow broker advisors the time to invest in detailed financial-planning issues. If annual sales targets are not maintained, their commission rates will be reduced, or they may even be fired.

We take the time to get to know our clients, and then we want them to come in at least annually for a review. This is far from a sales call, and it's not just small talk. It's important that we make a connection. As we forge a relationship, we are gaining a greater understanding that is crucial if we are to help you meet your objectives and goals.

Money is an emotional matter. Your thinking is not necessarily at its most rational when you are enamored of a second house or a luxury car that you would like to buy. If your children have a need, your parental sensibilities kick in. You want to help, but a loan might be much more appropriate than a gift. You should think twice about giving your money away when you might need it yourself during a long retirement. And any large gift above the annual exemption tax limit (according to the 2016 US Tax Code—$14,000) still needs to be documented properly for tax purposes. The best thing to do, if anything, depends upon your situation. These are times when you should seek your advisor's perspective and counsel. That's what a relationship is all about, and that's not what you will get from a salesperson.

THE RIGHT CHOICES

"If you make a bad bargain, hug it the tighter," Abraham Lincoln said, attributing it to advice from his father. He was not saying that we should refuse to correct poor choices. Nor was he suggesting that we should let ourselves sink ever deeper into losing endeavors. He was saying that we should honor our promises. He was espousing the importance of keeping a commitment.

Stubbornly clinging to a bad idea will result in failure. It's foolish to stay the course when it is leading you to a crash. That is a theme that you will encounter throughout this book, particularly when it comes to investments or choosing a financial advisor.

One must look at every decision in life as choosing wisely between the cherry and the pit. Despite his cynicism, the advice of that sales trainer years ago was unassailable. I just chose to give another meaning to the cherries in life.

CHAPTER 1

ENTERING NEW TERRITORY

To paraphrase the Italian Renaissance political theorist Niccolò Machiavelli, "The only thing permanent in life is change." Unfortunately, those who are in the best position to effect change are the ones least likely to do it.

Historically, those in power have favored the status quo. The serf had no say in the affairs of the kingdom. Today, the individual in free markets such as the United States *does* have the ability to make a difference. Collectively we can make changes in the government, and individually we can make something of ourselves. My father was a welder and my mother was a factory seamstress, and they worked to better their family. Through their guidance, my brother and sister and I gained an education that allowed us to maintain a higher standard of living.

In his book *Free to Choose*, the Nobel laureate Milton Friedman, one of the great economists of all time, describes how free-market capitalism did more to lift people from poverty than anything in the history of mankind. It opened opportunities—for those who chose to take them.

Along with ability comes obligation. To make things happen, you must act. If you don't change your course, you cannot get to a different destination. If we stay with the bad, our fortunes will get worse. If we want better, we need to move toward the good. Those who thrive are those who seek to improve themselves, to gain abilities, to get an education. Each of us can be a steward of change, if we accept the challenge. If we want what could be, we must pursue it.

No one can know everything or do it all alone. We need others to open our eyes and point us the right way. We must beware of the "things we don't know we don't know," as former Defense Secretary Donald Rumsfeld said. Or, in the words of Yogi Berra: "If you don't know where you're going, you might not get there."

It comes down to dealing effectively with the uncertainties of life. The path to success, however it's measured, requires that we see clearly.

LIFE IN THIRDS

The thirteenth-century Italian mathematician Fibonacci identified what has become to be known as the Fibonacci sequence of numbers, in which each is the sum of the previous two: 0, 1, 1, 2, 3, 5, 8, 13, 21, etc. This sequence is the determination of Fibonacci's golden ratio, 0.618, and 0.382, a principle of mathematics long known to architects, artists, and designers. In laymen's terms, it is the rule of thirds. Stock analysts view the Fibonacci pattern as a potential sign of reversal as stocks pull back by approximately a third, or sometimes two thirds, before rising again by a similar strength. The so-called herd mentality is nothing more than the mathematical pull of nature in human behavior. In nature specifically, these numeric patterns can be seen in the structure of such things as snail shells, tree branches, and the concentric swirls of sunflower seeds. It has been employed in economics and computer search algorithms. The code numbers used in the novel and movie *The Da Vinci Code* are an actual Fibonacci sequence.

This ratio also divides the course of a human life. Life comes in thirds. In our first thirty years, we are learning and getting direction, nurturing the seeds for what is to come. Our second thirty years is the time of growing and maturing. In our final thirty years, we are harvesting.

The rule of thirds is a significant consideration in retirement planning. We need to work within that natural division of our lives. During the accumulation stage, you should be establishing goals and determining how much money you will need to carry you the rest of the way. This is a stage of life when time is on your side. If you begin pursuing that course at age thirty, your savings and investments will be able to compound and grow for decades. If you wait until you are sixty, you have lost that time, and you cannot get it back.

Through compounding, a relatively small amount invested regularly over a long period will get you to your goal much more efficiently than trying to play catch-up at the end. The accumulation of wealth is based on a rather simple formula: the amount invested, times the number of years, times the rate of return. When you increase the number of years, the other two factors can be smaller to obtain the same result.

In other words: that second third of life, the accumulation stage, is the time to get serious about retirement goals. It is hard to accumulate much in the first third of life while striving to establish yourself and perhaps paying off student debt, but by about age thirty, the time of growth should be underway. The earlier, the better. If you wait too long, you could be in for a disappointing harvest—not the bountiful one that sensible planning and disciplined saving can provide.

Time can only work on your side when it has something to work on, and so you will need that money if you are to experience gains when the market rebounds. At age sixty, people with little in the way of savings cannot expect a bailout from a bull market. They can expect some unpleasant surprises, though, if they get super aggressive in investing what little they have. Be patient, and stay within your risk tolerance! A competent advisor will help you avoid emotional decisions and assist in keeping you in the game.

NOT WHAT YOU IMAGINED

Retirement is a mystery to most people. They have a picture in their heads of what life will be like when they enter this new territory, but it is mostly in the abstract. What they are likely to find will be somewhat different than they imagined—not necessarily worse, but probably in some ways surprising.

When people first retire, they often have a list of all the things they plan to do. "I'm going down to Home Depot to get what I need to fix the shed," or "I'm going to play golf twice a week." The first three days are a blur, and the first three months can feel like an extended vacation. And then reality sets in.

Retirement can be quite a psychological adjustment. On Friday, you were at work; you had a position of authority using your decades of experience. And then, on Monday, it's as if none of that mattered. You're not going back to work. You gained all that knowledge, and now it seems that nobody wants it. That's not easy.

The loss of one's work identity can be unsettling, and many people fail to anticipate that psychological adjustment. A few years back, I raced Porsches. I had a 911 with a manual six speed. This was not racing on an oval track. I raced on road tracks with constant stopping and turning. At one point you're zooming at 130 miles an hour, then you slow to fifty or twenty before accelerating into the turn. That's what you need to do in retirement. I recommend that people downshift by doing consulting work or whatever will help them to continue feeling productive. You need to be ready for Monday.

It also can be somewhat disconcerting when those paychecks cease. Perhaps you have a pension—although those are far fewer these days—and your Social Security benefit, plus some amount within a 401(k) or other tax-deferred retirement plan. If you have saved and invested, you might have a variety of other resources that could provide streams of income. But you cannot wait until the eve of retirement to start figuring all that out. You need to rally those resources to replace that paycheck. In fact, you should have been taking a hard look at those issues since you were fifty or even younger.

Proper planning makes all the difference between whether you will be heading into a retirement of struggle or of leisure. If you plan for your future, at least you can avoid those financial fears, and people identify the prospect of running out of money someday as their biggest concern when they retire.

Stress has its consequences. Marriages can crumble under the pressures, financial and otherwise, of retirement. Divorce can be particularly devastating during this third phase of life. Many retirees are in their second or third marriage, which statistics show to be more vulnerable even without this added strain. Often there are children on both sides from those previous marriages, which further complicates estate planning.

Divorce can be financially crippling. It drains the resources that could have grown into a healthy retirement fund. As painful as the process can be, this highlights the importance of working out the details in a prenuptial or shared-living agreement. The process forces people to sit down and talk about money and finances and how they will be handled. That communication alone can do much to dispel the future prospect of divorce. The adjustments of retirement can be stressful enough without adding a failed marriage to the mix.

A CHANGE OF FOCUS

My grandfather was born in 1886 and lived to be ninety-six years old. Once it was highly unusual to live so long, but it is becoming increasingly common. Centenarians are no longer rare in this age of medical advances.

A hundred and fifty years ago, many people didn't live beyond age forty-five. When the Social Security system was instituted in the 1930s, the typical age of mortality was sixty-five. That's why benefits did not begin until that age. The expectation was that most people would never collect, or collect only for a brief time.

Today, the combined life expectancy of men and women is approaching eighty. As the demographics change, the ramifications are immense. As people live longer thanks to better health care, they will depend increasingly upon that health care to sustain their quality of life. Bodies wear out, and the maintenance gets expensive.

And as we live longer, we need *more* money, not less! We need resources that will last as long as we do. That wasn't much of an issue when people worked until they died. Now they may continue to live as many years in retirement as they spent on the job. People are starting to understand that. The baby boomers are the first genera-tion to face en mass the daunting task of taking care of their elderly parents.

For young people, the focus tends to be on getting ahead. They are career oriented, trying to make a name for themselves and advance in their profession. Into their thirties and beyond, they work, produce, and contribute. Those middle years of life are a tremendous growth stage.

As the baby boomers have seen their parents live longer, they have become increasingly aware of the need to begin preparing for their own retirement years. Not only are they busy accumulating in these productive years, but they understand why they are doing it. They anticipate living to an age when they will be confronting a new set of challenges, much different from those they tackled in their growth years.

When pensions were the norm, people could put off such planning and perhaps pay few consequences. Now, by the time people are fifty, most are seeing the need to make a concerted effort to provide for their later years. The focus changes from trying to get ahead to trying to live well on what they set aside from their life's work.

COLLEGE VERSUS RETIREMENT

Those middle years also are the time of child rearing, and that becomes a significant strain on the family finances. It's not just the cost of diapers and blue jeans. Mom and dad begin to feel the weight of responsibility to launch their children into a productive adulthood. Most parents feel an obligation to start investing for those college days, and that obligation can severely crimp how much they are setting aside for their own retirement.

Most people in the accumulation years are pursuing two major financial goals: one is to save for the education of their children, and the other is to save for their retirement. Of course, comprehensive planning involves much more than that, but as people begin to put money aside, those are the two primary things on their minds.

Having established those goals, they set their objectives for reaching them. Goals and objectives are not synonymous terms. The goals are the destination; the objectives are the tools. To prepare for goals of the kids' tuition and their own retirement, the parents might set an objective to contribute regularly to their 401(k) or individual retirement account (IRA) or to obtain life insurance to cover the risk of premature death.

Unfortunately, satisfying both of those obligations can be a daunting endeavor. Nothing should stand in the way of the need to save for retirement, and once it was indeed quite possible to send children to college without losing that momentum. Today, however, paying for college has become a financial burden of monumental proportions.

When their children finally get out of college, the parents shift gears. Around the water cooler, they hear their colleagues chatting about retirement plans. They begin to wonder whether they have been saving enough for that big step. Most discover that they have not come close, and they have just spent a lot of money that would have gone a long way toward securing that day of financial independence.

Financial independence is simply a matter of reaching the point where you no longer need your paycheck to continue the same standard of living. That's what retirement is all about. It's not about buying a yacht and living in the Florida Keys or some other unrealistic image of the good life. Never mind those TV advertisements put out by the big financial institutions. Most of my clients just want to continue the same lifestyle that they have enjoyed for years, with the only difference being that they no longer need to go to work.

Most people certainly can attain that goal. It has become more difficult, however, in this era when college expenses have been competing for so many of the dollars that otherwise would have grown and compounded for retirement.

CONQUERING FEARS

There is still a sizable contingent of retirees who were children during the Great Depression and saw their parents struggling to put food on the table. Even if they were born after that difficult decade, they heard the stories of deprivation and desperation. Experiences such as that drill their way into the brain, and it is not surprising that so many people are afraid that they will run out of money. Even the very wealthy sometimes harbor that concern.

The two-earner household is now the norm, as women have entered the workforce in droves, a trend that began during World War II and the days of the "Rosie the Riveter" campaign to recruit female workers on the home front. It was a dramatic shift in the dynamics of the household. Both spouses have become the bread-winners, and for many this is not an optional arrangement. Couples worry about the loss of either income, and as they enter the unknown of retirement, they can feel the pressure even more acutely. They need more money to meet the higher standard of living that they have established.

The sad truth is that the average person has about $10,000 in savings at retirement. Lacking a pension, they depend upon their Social Security benefit and settle for a lower standard of living. And since financial independence is defined as maintaining that standard of living, they have failed to reach it.

So many things contribute to that failure to save sufficiently. The couple may have been making headway but suffered a loss in the stock market just as they were making a big withdrawal for those educational expenses, perhaps, or to pay for an elaborate wedding that some see as a daughter's birthright. Sometimes people thought they had saved enough but did not anticipate just how much taxes would drain their retirement income, or the extent that inflation would erode their purchasing power. Perhaps health issues sapped their savings, or they faced some unforeseen family emergency. Maybe a divorce dissipated their dollars and their dreams.

As you can see, the fear of running out of money often is quite founded. You certainly are not alone if you find yourself caught up in those concerns. You can conquer those worries by starting to save early and by planning thoroughly. I have dealt with many situations in my years in this business, and I have gained a sense of what works best for any particular predicament. I have helped countless people sort it all out. And I can say this with certainty: Whatever you have saved, it's time to think differently as you approach retirement. It's time to take a more protective stance to preserve the lifestyle that you worked so hard to attain.

CHAPTER 2

CREATING THE LIFE
YOU WANT

You may recall a scene in the movie *Dirty Harry* in which Clint Eastwood's character, Harry Callahan, blazes away at a group of bank robbers with his outsize six-shooter. As one of the wounded robbers scrambles for his dropped shotgun, Callahan takes aim with his revolver—and then, as the robber freezes, gives him a choice.

"I know what you're thinking: *Did he fire six shots or only five?*" Callahan tells him. "Well, to tell you the truth, in all this excitement, I've kinda lost track myself. But being this is a .44 Magnum, the most powerful handgun in the world, and would blow your head clean off, you've got to ask yourself one question: *Do I feel lucky?* Well, do ya, punk?" You can see the robber calculating his chances, and then he sides with reason.

Why am I relating this scene to you? Because it's a powerful illustration of the concept of game theory, a fascinating field to which MBA candidates are introduced in their studies of probability and statistics. You need to think ahead, assess the situation, calculate the odds, and plan your moves.

And as we find out in the film, two can play that game: As Callahan picks up the shotgun and starts to leave, the robber calls out, "Hey, I gotta know!" Dirty Harry turns and pulls the trigger. It clicks on an empty chamber, and he laughs as he walks away—a master at his craft.

Game theory is about decision making and strategy. How do you determine whether you should do one thing or the other? It's a principle of Monopoly and poker. It's the basis of football, baseball, and other sports. On another level, it's how politics, diplomacy, and warfare are conducted, both in the real world and in fantasy worlds, such as television's *Game of Thrones*.

So what does all this mean to you? It means that success involves much more than the hand that you're dealt. That's true in games, and that's true in deciding how to invest.

A CALCULATED STRATEGY

Creating the life you want requires a calculated strategy. First you set your goals, such as educating your children and preparing for a satisfying retirement. Then you establish your objectives for how you will get to those goals. What will be your tactics?

I have heard people who are unsure about an investment say, with a shrug, "Well, I'll just give it a shot." This is no time to play *Dirty Harry*. Calling it wrong could mean losing it all. When so much is at stake, it's better to play it safe, just like that bank robber. I usually can talk people down from such a risk, and I don't even have to say, "Do ya feel lucky, punk?"

Very few investors can play the game like a Warren Buffett or a Bill Gates. They are in a financial stratosphere that most people simply don't inhabit. When an investor is sitting on $40 billion in cash in a company, it's not about the money. It's strictly the game. Someone like that might hit it big on a $500,000 risk, but if he loses, so what? When most people lose that much, it's curtains.

Investing is not roulette. Roulette involves game theory, too, as does all gambling, but it's win or lose, black or red. That's not the way to invest. The odds must always be in the favor of the investor, who must strategize to manage risk. That's the orientation for success. Those who consistently guess wrong and make bad investments will be sorely lacking in retirement.

The period from 1982 to 2000 saw one of the greatest increases in stock prices since the stock market opened in 1796. People were making breathtaking returns. Those who retired in 1982 likely saw incredible success in those eighteen years. They could have withdrawn 4 percent of their portfolio for living expenses, year in and year out, and still have seen impressive gains in their original principal.

Now, let's fast-forward to look at what has happened to those who retired in 2000. If they have been withdrawing that same 4 percent annually, their scenario probably is quite different today. The huge declines in 2000, 2001, 2002, and again in 2008 were major drags on the fortunes of retirees. Many investors have seen little overall gain since 2000. As account values have declined, retirees' dreams have faded. They cannot escape the encroaching fear that their money might be running out . . . and they are only perhaps halfway through their retirement years.

It can be nearly impossible to recover from huge losses, particularly for people launching into retirement with a portfolio exposed to the market. In the 1990s, some investors were getting a 50 percent return and imagined that might continue forever—until they saw those stocks drop 80 percent by 2002. To get back to even from such a slam, you need an impossible 225 percent compounded gain, not an 80 percent gain as some might presume.

It takes more to get back to even than many people imagine. To erase a 50 percent loss requires a 100 percent gain. It's simple math: if you lose just 10 percent of $100, you'll be at $90. If you then gain 10 percent, you have only $99, not $100. If you started with a million dollars, you would have only $990,000. The pain worsens for multimillion-dollar accounts and greater percentages of loss. In 2008, some investors lost 40 percent, meaning $1 million was reduced to $600,000. After that market debacle, I saw the damage in the portfolios of people who came to me for help. Their broker/salesperson didn't know how to take action to minimize the decline. Their burden was unbearable.

Such are the cycles of our economy. The stock market did not recover from the 1929 crash until 1954. After the tech bubble burst in the late nineties, the NASDAQ didn't recover until 2014. You cannot control the equity market cycles, but you can understand that they will occur over many periods of your lifetime. Regardless of the cycle, you still need to invest for future goals. In fact, investing during market declines offers an opportunity to buy at lower prices and magnify the power of compounding. The important factor in the equation is continuing to invest, regardless of market behavior. There's an old Italian proverb: "You can't make bread without the flour."

Creating the life you want is about making the right decisions and making adjustments along the way. You will need to do so while dealing with circumstances that you cannot control. In other words, the economy will deal you a hand, and it's your responsibility to play it right. You must have a strategy for buying and selling securities.

If you have an advisor who never sells anything, you may have what I call an autopilot portfolio—and that can be deadly to retirement planning. Here's the problem: when a security goes south, sales-people who call themselves advisors will try to reassure their clients that all is well. "Just leave it alone," they will say. "It will come back." They really don't know how to protect the money (throw away the pits), but they say this nonetheless. If you're twenty years old, that might not be a problem. If you're sixty years old, you don't have that time to lose, particularly if you have just recovered from those recent periods of market turbulence. Not only did you lose principal, but you suffered the opportunity cost of what might have been if those lost dollars had been growing for you. For many, that was a stagger-ing double whammy that curtailed their retirement.

Knowledge is the antidote to such a dose of bad advice. To get ahead, we must associate with the right people, get the right infor-mation, and take the right actions. It requires more than wishful thinking about buying that boat or that beach house. You need a strategy to reach those goals, and you need to surround yourself with highly qualified people who will tell it like it is.

PLAYING THE HAND YOU'RE DEALT

The *Rule of Seventy-Two* is a simple formula that indicates how long it takes for money to double at a particular rate of return. If you divide seventy-two by the rate of return, the result is how many years it will take to double your money.

For example, if your return is 10 percent, then seventy-two divided by ten equals seven and two-tenth years. People who retired in the 1980s and who got that kind of return had the potential of seeing their money double twice before the market took a dive. That means $100,000 became $200,000, which became $400,000, without adding a nickel. Many people experienced such growth simply by virtue of the period in which they were investing.

When the roaring nineties were over, investors were soon to see two severe equity bear markets, defined as a decline of 20 percent or more. The average person doesn't anticipate such a period of no growth or sluggish growth, but it was the nature of the times. The investors didn't cause the downturns, but they certainly needed to be ready for them and to adjust to them. Investors must take strategic action to avoid losing their money and, along with it, the cost of so much lost opportunity.

You can point fingers at Wall Street, at the government, and at the Federal Reserve, and you can rail about derivatives and the quasi-government entities Fannie Mae and Freddie Mac that provided the mortgage money to the banks, and you can reassure yourself that none of that was your fault. And it wasn't. The government was just as culpable as Wall Street. Does anyone really get their money back when the Federal Reserve throws money out of helicopters, as they did for the banks after 2008?

Nonetheless, those were the cards that investors were dealt. You may still be holding some of those cards. How will you play them? The principles of game theory highlight the need for a careful strategy, whether the game is investing or poker or baseball. As of 2016, we are perhaps only in the fifth inning of this recovery game. Have central bankers worldwide now created a future debt crisis after years of monetary stimulus? One problem has led to another. Now, we are dealing with near-zero interest rates, meaning that retirement strategies must deal with the prospect of several years of a depressed bond market. In 1982, according to StockCharts data, the interest rate on the ten-year US Treasury bond was 16 percent; in early 2016, it was just 1.8 percent. Money-market funds used to pay 4 percent annually; now they pay 0.1 percent. The game goes on.

You may be wondering what you're supposed to do about all that—throw up your hands, whine, complain, and feel sorry for yourself? Rest assured that there are things you can do. To make the right moves requires an understanding of the playing field.

Most advisors, for example, are totally unaware of the huge correction that is coming in the bond market, in which we may be seeing negative total returns (interest rate minus the price of the security) for years to come. Some still hold to an outdated and ill-advised principle known as the *Rule of 100*, which suggests the percentage of bonds in a portfolio should be about the same number as the investor's age. In other words, a seventy-year-old would have a portfolio composed of 70 percent bonds and 30 percent equities.

That could be challenging and ineffective in our current economic climate. Bond prices drop as interest rates rise—and since interest rates can scarcely get much lower, their future direction is pretty much a given. And yet, believe it or not, new clients still have been coming to me with 40 or 50 percent of their portfolio invested in traditional corporate and Treasury bonds. These are the portfolios produced by the "advisors" in the large brokerage houses that advertise heavily to the baby-boomer generation. I'm appalled by what I see.

PURSUIT WITH PURPOSE

You should not just be ambling along, whether in life or in your investments. You need to pursue with a purpose. Sigmund Freud suggested that it is our ability to love and work that is fundamental to happiness. Happy people are those who have good relationships and who are doing work that they enjoy.

In essence, that is the life that we all want. We are social animals who have long since come out of the cave. When those two elements are working well for us, we can properly put our plans in place. Some dream of luxuries, but most people want more modest joys. Most of the "millionaires next door" want simple things, family things. Some of my clients need $200,000 a year, and some can live on $30,000 a year. Either way can be fine when the level of spending is within their reach. Problems only arise with overreaching—and that is why you should work with someone to track that spending. Positive cash flow (i.e., more money coming in than going out) is good this year, but will it continue for the next twenty years? Figure 2.1 shows a plan that will not work over time. Inflows and outflows have to match. Figure 2.2 shows in detail that if the problems are not addressed early, money will not support as comfortable a retirement. Inflation and taxes are the stealth factors that affect both inflows and outflows.

If you are not getting that help, you are at risk of either overspending or underspending. If you are inclined to overspend and take excess money out of your portfolio, you have stamped upon it the date when it no longer can grow. It no longer will be working for you. It no longer will be compounding. In fact, it will be de-compounding. Underspending is better than overspending, of course, but if unwarranted fear is motivating that frugality, you could end up dying with millions in your account. Or someday, when it is too late to enjoy that money, the regrets will set in: "Why, oh why, didn't we take that trip with the kids?"

It comes down to getting a grip on your priorities, to defining the life you want and going after it. This needs to begin during your accumulation years. Saving for retirement certainly needs to be one of your prime goals, against which you weigh the others. If you decide that sending your children to college is a high priority, for example, then you need to work on both goals at the same time. If you focus only on funding their tuition, it will be at the expense of funding your retirement—and that's too much of a sacrifice. It would help everyone at all income levels if colleges reduced their degree requirements from four years to three, but I doubt the academic cartel would agree to such a radical but sensible idea. Again, it's not something we can control.

INFLOWS AND OUTFLOWS

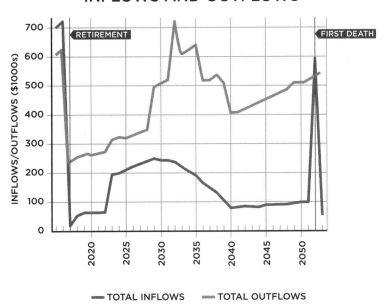

PORTFOLIO ASSETS

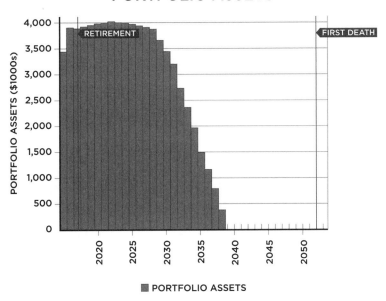

Fig. 2.1

Cash Flow

Base Facts (All Years)
Prepared for Mr. & Mrs. Sample

The Cash Flow report illustrates your income, savings, expenses, and resulting net cash flow on an annual basis.

Year	Age	Income Flows	Investment Income	Planned Distributions	Other Inflows	Total Inflows	Total Expenses	Planned Savings	Total Outflows	Net Cash Flow	Total Portfolio Assets
2015	63/62	$700,000	$0	$0	$0	$700,000	$559,649	$48,000	$607,649	$92,351	$3,447,513
2016	64/63	717,500	0	0	0	717,500	573,704	49,000	622,704	94,796	3,903,769
2017	65/64	9,997	0	0	0	9,997	234,858	0	234,858	(224,861)	3,896,933
2018	66/65	48,060	0	0	0	48,060	251,971	0	251,971	(203,911)	3,922,505
2019	67/66	57,722	0	0	0	57,722	260,556	0	260,556	(202,834)	3,952,241
2020	68/67	58,587	0	0	0	58,587	263,223	0	263,223	(204,636)	3,981,920
2021	69/68	59,465	0	0	0	59,465	265,965	0	265,965	(206,500)	4,011,526
2022	70/69	60,356	0	0	0	60,356	268,638	0	268,638	(208,282)	4,041,093
2023	71/70	61,262	0	131,526	0	192,788	312,177	0	312,177	(119,389)	4,029,763
2024	72/71	62,181	0	139,114	0	201,295	318,673	0	318,673	(117,378)	4,012,103
2025	73/72	63,113	0	147,132	0	210,245	321,320	0	321,320	(111,075)	3,991,660
2026	74/73	64,060	0	155,602	0	219,662	328,425	0	328,425	(108,763)	3,963,826
2027	75/74	65,021	0	164,547	0	229,568	335,801	0	335,801	(106,233)	3,927,898
2028	76/75	65,996	0	173,993	0	239,989	347,456	0	347,456	(107,467)	3,879,130
2029	77/76	66,986	0	179,979	0	246,965	494,434	0	494,434	(247,469)	3,681,429
2030	78/77	67,991	0	177,771	0	245,762	504,712	0	504,712	(258,950)	3,462,538
2031	79/78	69,011	0	173,929	0	242,940	516,863	0	516,863	(273,923)	3,219,471
2032	80/79	70,046	0	168,229	0	238,275	727,217	0	727,217	(488,942)	2,752,599
2033	81/80	71,096	0	149,427	0	220,523	608,451	0	608,451	(387,928)	2,377,649
2034	82/81	72,163	0	134,399	0	206,562	624,093	0	624,093	(417,531)	1,965,867
2035	83/82	73,245	0	115,557	0	188,802	639,235	0	639,235	(450,433)	1,515,506
2036	84/83	74,344	0	92,278	0	166,622	511,648	0	511,648	(345,026)	1,167,020
2037	85/84	75,459	0	73,166	0	148,625	519,221	0	519,221	(370,596)	791,190
2038	86/85	76,591	0	51,011	0	127,602	534,452	0	534,452	(406,850)	379,131
2039	87/86	77,740	0	24,319	0	102,059	506,175	0	506,175	(404,116)	(27,998)
2040	88/87	78,906	0	0	0	78,906	401,591	0	401,591	(322,685)	(349,756)
2041	89/88	80,090	0	0	0	80,090	411,344	0	411,344	(331,254)	(680,060)
2042	90/89	81,291	0	0	0	81,291	421,342	0	421,342	(340,051)	(1,019,137)
2043	91/90	82,511	0	0	0	82,511	431,590	0	431,590	(349,079)	(1,367,218)
2044	92/91	83,749	0	0	0	83,749	442,093	0	442,093	(358,344)	(1,724,539)
2045	93/92	85,005	0	0	0	85,005	452,860	0	452,860	(367,855)	(2,091,345)
2046	94/93	86,281	0	0	0	86,281	463,894	0	463,894	(377,613)	(2,467,883)
2047	95/94	87,575	0	0	0	87,575	475,205	0	475,205	(387,630)	(2,854,411)
2048	96/95	88,888	0	0	0	88,888	486,809	0	486,809	(397,921)	(3,251,203)
2049	97/96	90,222	0	0	0	90,222	498,707	0	498,707	(408,485)	(3,658,530)
2050	98/97	91,575	0	0	0	91,575	510,903	0	510,903	(419,328)	(4,076,671)

This analysis must be reviewed in conjunction with the limitations and conditions disclosed in the Disclaimer page. Projections are based on assumptions provided by the advisor/representative and are not guaranteed. Actual results will vary, perhaps to a significant degree. The projected reports are hypothetical in nature and for illustrative purposes only. Return assumptions do not reflect the deduction of any commissions. They will reflect any fees or product charges when entered by the advisor/representative. Deduction of such charges would result in a lower rate of return. Consult your legal and/or tax advisor before implementing any tax or legal strategies.

Fig. 2.2 | Running out of money at ages 88/87 is not a good plan.

GETTING ORGANIZED

People hate paperwork, virtually without exception. They scramble in March trying to get together everything they will need to take to the accountant at tax time, and the documents are scattered in various drawers. "Just make a file folder," I suggest to them, "and throughout the year put into it anything that is tax sensitive as it comes your way. That way it will all be there, and you can just hand the folder to your accountant so you won't go crazy."

That is also a good approach to organizing your documents for financial planning. You and your advisor need access to all of that information so that it can be considered as a whole. To create the life that you want, you have to get organized. Not only do you need to get your priorities in order, but you need to get those documents in order.

Financial planning encompasses your net worth, which is your assets minus your liabilities, so you need full documentation of that. It involves tax management, so your tax returns will provide a wealth of information. It involves an analysis of your cash flow—of the money in, money out. Your advisor also will be looking at your investments, of course, and at your insurance coverage. How much have you been setting aside for retirement and for educating your children? That's all under the financial-planning umbrella, too, as well as trusts and wills and other documents of estate planning.

All of those elements of financial planning should be regularly monitored. Most people take the approach of looking at just one area at a time. An accountant isn't enough. For individuals, accountants normally just look at taxes. A lawyer will deal with your legal matters, such as your estate documents. A stockbroker will be happy to look at your investments. They each have their role, but to plan effectively, you need to look horizontally across all those areas, not just vertically at one.

Most people do not have the time, inclination, or training to do this as thoroughly as is necessary. A CFP® will help to keep track of all those aspects, without conflict of interest, to monitor how they interrelate. Unless they all are functioning in concert, your financial plan won't work. Some areas, of course, will need more regular attention than others, such as investments and taxes, but they all require at least annual review. That is why it is so important that the documents be organized and readily accessible. The Internet and interactive-planning software today allow an easier path for both client and advisor to keep information current.

A TIME FOR VIGILANCE

Effective financial planning requires starting with the end in mind. Before choosing your investments, you need to know what you are hoping to accomplish with those investments. Once you know that, you can put in place the various strategies essential for success, fine-tuning your financial plan to stay on track toward your goals.

This is no place for those autopilot portfolios from a stockbroker or for those impersonal and inhuman robo-advisors. With those, nobody is minding the store. The asset allocation essentially comes right out of a book. You will have some percentage of each of the four major asset classes—stocks, bonds, commodities, and commercial real estate—but there are times when conditions require adjustments. If nobody is paying attention, there go your dreams.

Instead, this is the place for an advisor of vigilance who will watch the positions in your portfolio every day to determine whether your investment strategy is reacting properly according to market conditions. This is the place for an advisor who will help you assess the results in the context of your life goals. This is the place for someone who knows the cherries from the pits. You and your portfolio deserve nothing less.

CHAPTER 3

BEHIND DOOR
NUMBER ONE . . .

You're standing in front of the studio audience, staring at the three curtains on stage as Monty Hall (or for today's viewers, Wayne Brady) holds the microphone close to your face and the glittery lady waits to open one to reveal your prize. Behind one is a new car! Behind another, a dining room set! And behind the third curtain—a pig.

And now, *Let's Make a Deal!* It's decision time: Will it be door number one, two, or three? And then Monty tells you that he can take away all that pressure, and you can simply accept $1,000 right now, on the spot. What will you do?

Such is the way many people invest. It's a matter of probability and statistics. Two of those curtains are good, so you have a 67 percent probability of winning. So why do some people go for the thousand bucks? This is the concept of loss aversion; the fear of loss tends to be greater than the joy of gain. That's a fact of the human condition. Even with a high probability of doing well, people fear picking the pig.

In the movie *Rebel Without a Cause*, two teenagers, one played by James Dean, play a deadly game of "chicken" as they race their cars toward a cliff. The first to lose his nerve and jump out of the speeding car will be the loser. In other words, winning requires, in this case, a high risk of loss. After all, when there is a cliff involved, assets tend to plunge and crash when they go off the edge.

When it comes to the market, which has also been known to crash, some people say that they would never, ever, take such a chance. Others say that they might, but not now, not yet; it's just not the right time. And others say, "Sure, I think I can do that—let's go for it!" Investors come with a range of risk tolerances.

My point is this: you're playing a dangerous game if you wait too long to consider your retirement goals and how much money you will need to reach them. You easily can get too close to the edge, to the point where you're not going to make it. Your sleeve can get caught in the door latch at the worst possible time, and off you go, over the cliff.

The unexpected happens, even when you are cocksure about yourself. It's that rule of self-exception again, where bad things only happen to the other guy, and it is particularly striking among the young who sometimes feel immortal. Not so when you're fifty. Most people are taking precautions and planning ahead by then. But if you wait until you are sixty to start thinking about retirement, you could be doomed. The formulas will no longer work for you. You cannot gain much advantage from compounding, not with only a few years left in the race.

NO MORE GOLD WATCHES

In the old days, it seemed everybody got a gold watch upon retiring. Today, with the price of gold recently at about $1,100 an ounce, the boss says so long with a handshake. Not only do you not get that gold watch, but it's just as unlikely that the company will be giving you that generous pension. Those *defined-benefit* plans, which so many people once depended upon for a reliable retirement income, are nearing extinction. In the 1950s, about 80 percent of workers got a pension. Today, that's fewer than 15 percent, and falling. Many of the ones that remain are underfunded and in danger of collapse, especially in the public-government sector (your tax dollars at work).

With the passing of the defined-benefit pensions, we have seen the rise of the 401(k)s and similar retirement accounts known as *defined-contribution* plans, in which the employee saves money, possibly with a company match. It's up to the worker whether to save, unlike the pension system in which employers were required by statute to make regular contributions. In short, the onus of saving and investing for retirement has shifted from the employer to the employee.

That fundamental shift in the underlying structure of retirement planning doesn't have to be a bad thing at all, but it does mean that the individual must start investing early, contributing as much as possible. Most people feel that they cannot spare, say, 15 percent of their salary, for one reason or another. Then they get to age sixty and say, "Oh my God, I don't have enough money, I'd better start saving 15 percent of my salary!" A lack of education in these issues doesn't change the reality of the situation: saving for retirement is a responsibility that pensioners didn't necessarily need to consider.

A smart approach is to start by saving perhaps 2 percent at age thirty, and then each year raising the 401(k) contribution by 1 percentage point until you reach the maximum that the plan allows. With such a small increment, you will not miss the money, as you would if you tried to increase your contribution by 5 percentage points all at once. Plus, the money comes right out of your paycheck, so you won't have the temptation or opportunity to spend it. It's a voluntary *forced-savings plan* that works because you don't have to think about it.

These plans also offer a tremendous tax break because contributions are not taxed up front. They are not counted as part of your salary, and so you get that immediate deduction. This amounts to getting free money from the government. If you decline to participate in a 401(k) plan, you're making a big mistake. You get an immediate tax savings of $1,000 if you are in the 25 percent marginal tax bracket and you contribute $4,000. Why wouldn't you do that? Look at it another way: the government wants to give you $1,000— do you want it?

Maybe it's because no one told you what a deal you were getting. Your human resources department is not about to become your personal planner. In fact, the Department of Labor frowns upon employers getting involved in the choices that employees make in their 401(k) plans. That's *your* responsibility. Whether you save, and how you save, is not the purview of the company or the plan advisor, who may be made up of robo-advisors, many fresh out of college.

Once your money is in the 401(k) plan, it should be there to stay until retirement, when you can withdraw it at the prevailing tax rate at the time. If you withdraw it earlier than age fifty-nine and a half, you will be charged a 10 percent penalty, along with ordinary income tax rates.

There are hardship provisions that allow 401(k) participants to borrow from the plan. From a planning perspective, however, doing so is a bad idea unless you are truly in financial difficulty and can take the money as a loan, paying yourself back with interest. What I find troubling is the opportunity cost that people pay when they take that step. The sum that they withdraw no longer is working for them. Yes, you are paying yourself back, but are you getting closer to your retirement goal? Opportunity cost and the power of compounding are sacrificed.

Instead of borrowing from a 401(k) plan, particularly for people in their fifties, I recommend instead that they take out a home equity line of credit or get a loan at the bank. The retirement money should remain targeted to that goal. Psychologically, people feel more responsible to pay back a bank loan even though a 401(k) withdrawal might seem easier.

Frankly, most people need a coach who will say, "Look, that's not a good idea, and here's why." Good advisors will not make you do anything. Instead, they will explain the options and consequences. They will tell you how one thing affects another. You will be able to make your decisions based on information that you might not have understood on your own. That's a relationship that goes far beyond urging you to buy this stock or that bond.

SIZING UP SOCIAL SECURITY

Along with the loss of their pensions, many people feel far less secure about their Social Security benefits. In the early days of the system, about eight workers contributed for every one retiree receiving a benefit. The ratio now is about two to one, and the baby boomers have only just started into their retirement years. In time, it will be one to one—and even negative in contributions. It's not hard to see why that is not sustainable. This much is certain: things will change. The system will be different than it is today for people retiring twenty years from now.

Generally, whenever the government alters the Social Security system, the changes affect only people younger than fifty-five. At some point, the standard retirement age will be rising to seventy, but when Congress takes that step, anyone fifty-five or older probably will not be affected. Social Security is the third rail of politics: the politicians are careful about touching it because they know they can get zapped. A lot of baby boomers are retiring, and they also are voting.

Among the first retirement decisions that people must make is when to switch on their Social Security benefit. And the answer is: *it depends*. No two households are the same, and that is yet one more reason why it is so important to consult with someone who has experience in these matters.

The decision to turn on Social Security is an emotional one for many people because it feels as if they have crossed the threshold. Besides being psychological, the decision, of course, is also largely a financial one. The income that you earn on the job now must come from somewhere else. That means retirees need to take a hard look at the streams of income that will sustain them.

For many, that has meant their pension payments and their Social Security benefit, primarily. But as we have seen, those pensions are getting rare. Social Security in itself is a form of a defined-benefit pension, in that you get a stream of income without having access to the principal. You don't get a lump sum, as you might get under defined-contribution or 401(k)-type pension plans. Nor, when you are working, do you ordinarily have access to the company's money. You are living on your earnings. That is the kind of cash flow to which most people have been accustomed all their working lives.

Because it is a reliable source of such regular cash flow, the Social Security is important; the benefit cannot be discounted in retirement planning. It comes every month and goes directly into your bank account. Today, the full retirement age is sixty-six to sixty-seven, depending upon when you were born. The government has made adjustments to that age and is likely to do so again in its continuing attempts to shore up the Social Security system, which is underfunded for future retirees.

The discussion on when it's best to switch on your benefit can be long and involved, but essentially you should take it when you need it. To a large extent, that will depend upon your health. Frankly, a big part of the decision hinges on how long you expect that you and your spouse might live. Ideally, if you are in reasonably good health, it's a good idea to wait until you are at full-retirement age or later. For every year that you postpone the benefit, it will increase by about 8 percent, all the way up to age seventy.

When people ask whether they should apply for Social Security immediately or wait awhile, I ask them two questions. The first is: "Do you need the money?" Often they tell me they do not because they or their spouse is still working, or they have a pension, or they have an inheritance, or many other reasons. Then I ask, "How is your health?" If all is well there, I suggest they wait before collecting.

However, if they need the money, and their health issues go far beyond the usual aches and pains of getting older, I suggest that they apply sooner rather than later—at age sixty-six or even sixty-two. There's an old expression: "A bird in hand is worth two in the bush." If you have serious health issues that could cut your life short, collect your money while you can.

Another option—and one that people seldom talk about—is this: if you are at full-retirement age and don't need the money because you still are working, consider collecting your benefit and then investing it. Let's say you are due about $25,000 a year. By the age of seventy, you will have received $100,000 from the Social Security system. If you invest that money regularly rather than spend it, and if the market cooperates, you could end up with considerably more than that, perhaps $110,000.

That can offset the fact that you would have had a larger monthly payment if you had waited until seventy to begin collecting. And now you have an account that you can use at your discretion, or let it continue to grow as a bequest for your heirs.

However, I suggest that you do take your benefit if your only alternative is to start withdrawing from your investment account. Whatever you get in Social Security will be that much less that you will need to withdraw. If postponing your benefit would mean that you would be draining your investment principal, then you should claim your benefit.

WEIGHING PENSION OPTIONS

If you still are eligible to receive a pension, the choices can get complicated. Should you take a lump sum, if it is offered? Should you opt for the full monthly payment, which would mean your spouse would get nothing if you died first? Should you accept a 10 percent lower payment so that your spouse would continue to have a 50 percent survivor benefit? Maybe you are thinking about choosing a 20 percent reduction so your spouse would continue receiving the same monthly payment. No matter your choice, the decision is *irrevocable*. You can't change it once the signature is notarized.

It's like choosing between door number one, two, or three. Any of those choices could be good or bad, depending upon your circumstances and needs. How is your health? How is the health of your spouse, and is he or she likely to outlive you? Those are just a few of the variables. All of the options can be weighed and calculated, but left to your own devices, you are likely to lean on emotions. You might be tempted to give up far too much, for example, because you are afraid and therefore overcompensate to cover your risks. That's when your decision is most likely to go off course.

A good advisor can help to get things in perspective. Perhaps you have an insurance policy that could go to your spouse upon your death; that way, the risk is covered and you could take the higher pension payment for a greater lifetime income. Or perhaps your other investments are quite sufficient to take care of your spouse if you were to pass early. If that's the case, why not take the maximum now, if it's offered?

The company probably would prefer a lump-sum distribution. It costs the company hundreds of dollars a year for every person still in the pension plan. The third-party administrators, who essentially are the accountants of the pension plan, charge the company to track the retirees and keep them on the books. That's why the company would rather say, "Here's a check, and good-bye."

I like the idea of that "take the money and run" option. You gain the freedom to choose how you will use the lump sum, though along with that freedom comes the responsibility to manage it wisely. Ideally you should nurture it and grow it. Not only could you bolster your retirement income, but you might also have something to leave to the next generation.

Unfortunately, for some people, that lump sum burns a hole in the pocket. They start to spend down the principal. It's as if they cannot control themselves. Most people, however, will do well to accept the lump sum so long as they maintain the discipline to make the money last. That requires consulting with someone who understands the issues, appropriately invests the money, and monitors the annual cash flow.

A MATTER OF MOMENTUM

The fear of loss is part of the human condition of risk aversion. Much of it is instinctive, but it can also be a learned behavior. Think of those who were scarred by the Great Depression, or more recently by what some have dubbed the Great Recession. Certainly, the experiences of recent years have contributed to an increase in loss aversion.

The investing concept of "absolute momentum," championed by Gary Antonacci, author of *Dual Momentum Investing*, can play well in that atmosphere. For investment growth, you want to gain momentum on the upside and avoid it on the downside. When your positions are falling, they will reach a point that is absolute. We call that the trigger point, and that is when it may be time to sell.

Recognizing that trigger point of absolute momentum requires training and experience. One simple measure, along with a variety of others, is to examine the one-year chart. If the momentum of a security has been negative for one year, it is likely that something is inherently wrong.

Most investors react emotionally and do not understand when to sell. A company such as Vanguard or Fidelity, the two biggest self-directed custodians, will not provide advice on whether to sell. They're just providers. They won't take on the liability of giving advice. And most advisors do not have a clue when to sell. Buying is easy; anyone can do it, especially in a bull market. Selling is hard. It requires a "process" that is not emotionally driven but is based on statistical factors. It doesn't have to work all the time, but it prevents losses such as we witnessed in 2008 *(see fig. 3.1)*.

Yes, anyone can seem to be doing well when the market is rallying. There's an old expression: "Everyone is a genius in a bull market." Until it's a bear market. Back in the late 1990s, a client called me, eager to buy Yahoo stock. "My friends are buying it," he

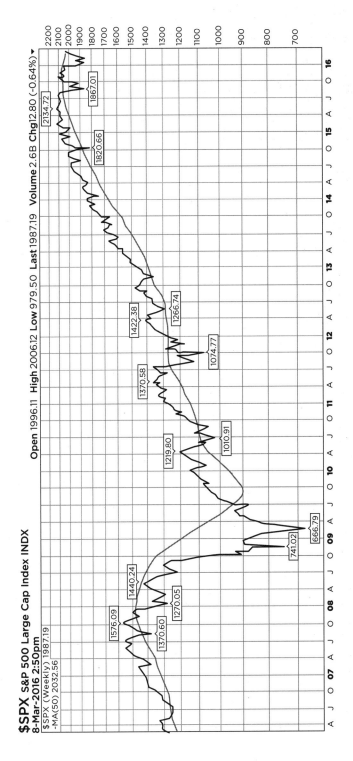

Fig. 3.1 | There are times when selling is required to reduce portfolio risk.

explained. "It's up double this year!" Fundamentally, the company didn't have any earnings. It had a ridiculously high price-earnings ratio of 1500:1. To put that in perspective, the S&P 500 ratio in 2015 was about 18:1, which analysts see as historically pricey.

"I'm not going to invest your money like that," I told my client. He insisted on buying into Yahoo, so I suggested that he put some money into a separate account for which he would be solely responsible. He did. And in 2000, he lost most of his money. He didn't blame me. He knew it was his own fault. When value is distorted, it is best to stay away.

The key is to determine when it's time to sell. Determining that point is the essence of any momentum strategy. It is one of many sell disciplines, but the one-year point is a serious time line for consideration.

Let's look at an example: According to StockCharts, in 2000, Microsoft was priced at its high point of $42.32 per share, just before the tech market started to collapse. It was not until December 2014 that Microsoft got back to $42.32. Those who held on to that stock suffered a huge opportunity cost in those fourteen years.

"I'll just leave it alone, it'll bounce back," some people say when an investment has turned sharply south, to which a reasonable response is, "How do you know?" I recall telling a client that he really should sell his WorldCom stock because of the downward momentum. He sold out at $60 a share. WorldCom eventually went to zero.

If you ever wonder how far down a stock can go, the answer is to zero! I warned another client to divest himself of his Concurrent Computer shares. "No, no, it'll come back," he said. It didn't. It went to zero, and it was 75 percent of his portfolio.

According to StockCharts data, at the beginning of 2008, Citicorp, one of the great banking financial institutions, was at $229 a share. It dropped to $9.64. Some of the Citicorp executives who had most of their money tied up in their company lost their life savings. Did the stock ever bounce back? Not much. As of November 2015, Citicorp stock was at $60.84.

When would have been a good time to sell those stocks as they fell? An astute advisor who has a sell discipline—and most do not— would be able to help you analyze the momentum in such situations. To avoid getting into predicaments like those, you need to cut your risk. That doesn't stop you from buying back in at some point, as the market permits. But during corrections, when the market is pulling down in the 5 to 10 percent range, it's a sensible strategy to take some profits and start reducing some positions *(see fig. 3.2)*. Every bear market starts with a 10 percent correction. Once the market hits a 20 percent decline, which is the definition of a bear market, you don't know how far down it might go. In 2008, the S&P dropped 38 percent, and commercial real estate dropped 60 percent. In 2000, the NASDAQ dropped 80 percent.

The discipline of momentum and other factors are integral in determining the point when a security position should be reduced. Not all asset classes are the same. The four asset classes of stocks, bonds, commodities, and commercial real estate investment trusts (REITs) operate with different cash flows, and within those asset classes are more defined sectors. Through intermarket analysis, we monitor asset-class changes. When interest rates go down, for example, stocks and bonds generally do well. When interest rates are rising, three of those asset classes tend not to work well. The exception is stocks, which can do well in either climate. Of course this is simplistic and only a general rule.

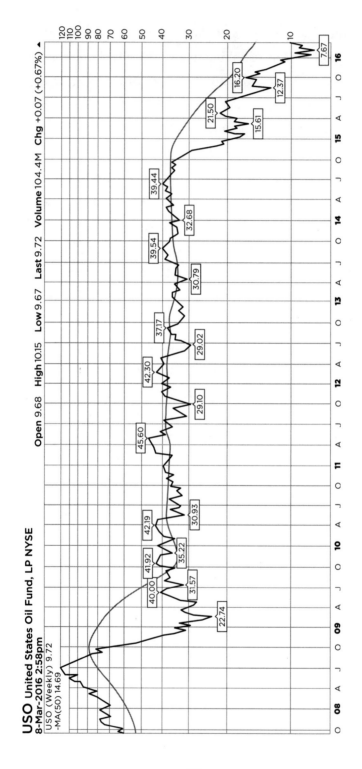

Fig. 3.2 | USO—Exchange Traded Fund of the commodity oil.

Oil was a good buy as it ran up to $150/barrel, but were you advised to hold it as it dropped to $9.00 in 2016?

Interest rates and bond prices have an inverse relationship: as one is falling, the other is rising. In recent times, falling interest rates produced a bull market in bonds. In 1982, the ten-year Treasury bond yielded 16 percent, but those yields have come down dramatically in the decades since. As a natural result, bond prices have risen. In a climate of very low interest rates, yields are likely to swing upward. We have seen the clear beginning of that trend. How it plays out in the next five or ten years is uncertain, and that is the nature of the marketplace.

That uncertainty also highlights the danger of dealing with salespeople who lack a sell discipline. They do not understand intermarket analysis. Certain positions of a portfolio are likely to break down independently of other positions. It is not just about the S&P 500 and the Dow Jones Industrial Average indices. You need a process that monitors and anticipates the price changes of your positions. If your decisions are based on the probabilities, you will get it right most of the time. That is what investing is all about.

As you get close to retirement, protection of principal is the name of the game. You cannot take excessive risk and lose money, because you don't have enough time to catch up. Holding on too long to a losing position puts your principal in peril. With so much at stake, you cannot be guessing at what lies behind which door. This is no time for wishful thinking. This is the time for a careful and calculated strategy.

CHAPTER 4

THE PILOT BESIDE ME

Once when I was on a flight to a business meeting, I took a seat next to a gentleman in uniform. He clearly was a pilot. Airlines often let their pilots travel wherever they wish as a passenger if there's an open seat.

We began to chat, and he told me that he piloted 747s. "How does that feel," I asked him, "to be responsible for the lives of hundreds of people behind you on that plane?"

"Well," he said with a half-smile, "I'm up there in the front of the plane."

That pilot understood the very clear fact that his responsibility for every person on a plane also included the people in the cockpit. To give his passengers the smoothest ride possible meant doing the same thing for himself.

You won't find many people on an airplane who feel they could replace the pilot. They don't want that job. They hold no illusions that they could do that job. They just want the reassurance that the leader up front is competent and capable of getting them to their destination.

Likewise, financial-planning clients should be looking for a competent advisor who is capable of getting them to their destination. Often the sign of good advisors is that they invest their own money similarly to the way they invest their clients' money. Yes, the advisor certainly might have a different personal risk level than some of those clients, but overall it's certainly cause for concern when advisors don't practice what they preach.

Most mutual-fund managers do invest in their own fund. In fact, the Securities and Exchange Commission and the Financial Industry Regulatory Authority prohibit the practice of "front running": advisors cannot buy a security for themselves before they buy it for their clients, unless they can document a valid reason. If not, they can be fined and disciplined for doing so. Ethical advisors take the same responsibility for their clients' money as they would their own money.

GATHERERS VS. MANAGERS

Charles de Vaulx, advisor for the IVA Worldwide Fund, had this to say in a recent Barron's article: "At the end of the day, one has to decide whether one is, first and foremost, in the asset-gathering business or in the money-management business."

Salespeople are in the asset-gathering business. They work on behalf of their company to pull in investments. That is their focus. They are not in the money-management business. They don't manage anything. They outsource that aspect, and they're not paying much attention to it. Instead, they are out looking for more sales, gathering more assets.

I am firmly in the camp of the money managers. Like the pilot I met on that flight, I take full responsibility for the welfare of those who choose to come along with me for the ride. Their best interest is my best interest. It is the definition of fiduciary. We are aligned in our desire to make the most of their portfolios and their financial plans for a fulfilling retirement.

It is not as simple as placing client assets into a 40/60 percent mix of equities and bonds, for example—and pretend that does an adequate job of covering risk. You can't make it safely to your destination on autopilot. I actually get up into the cockpit, examine the gauges, and take hold of the controls. Someone has to guide that financial plane in for a landing.

That's a responsibility that requires experience, skill, good judgment, and close attention. You need the right advisor for the job, one with the proper training. You need a money manager. You don't want an asset gatherer who puts your assets in an autopilot structure so he or she doesn't have to monitor the positions daily, weekly, or even monthly. Sure, it works in a booming business cycle, as industries ramp up and consumers open their wallets and the economy looks bright. But then production overtakes demand, and the economy starts to drift as businesses cut sharply back. That's when you need a sell discipline to prevent your portfolio from imploding.

You need to be working with somebody who understands the long-term cycles and will monitor the shifts in market trends. Momentum shifts do not happen quickly but over weeks and months. Eventually, the process will signal the need to sell or to reallocate to a position appropriate for the circumstances.

Business cycles rise and fall like an ocean wave. No one can predict with precision the strength of each wave and how long it will last. We have had market cycles as long as thirty-five years, in the wake of the crash that heralded the Great Depression. On average, however, business cycles have lasted about five years, going through expansions and contractions. As I write this, we are in the seventh year of an expansion that began when the market bottomed out dramatically in 2009.

I'm not suggesting that we are in for another crash or a long decline. I'm suggesting that investors should look at the indicators and make the necessary moves to preserve a healthy portfolio. It is crucial during these cycles to make regular adjustments. Salespeople will not provide the necessary guidance.

Nor will you get good advice from the media. You certainly can get a lot of noise from the media. Some of those self-help money publications have been dubbed "financial pornography," and for good reason. The so-called advice gets ridiculous. And by the time the magazines, and even the Internet nabobs, are chattering about some latest hot tip, it's too late for the typical investor. With modern, high-frequency computer programs trading at one hundred trades per second, there is no such thing as catching a hot-tip.

The Three Camels

Long ago at a conference of financial salespeople, I heard a speaker tell a tale about a man who wanted to cross the desert, and he interviewed three camels who seemed to be likely prospects for the journey. He asked the first camel, "How many bags of oats would you need to cross the desert?" The camel answered, "Ten." He asked the second camel the same question. "Nine," said the camel. And finally he asked the third camel, who answered, "Five." The man was incredulous. "Only five bags? That's impossible. You'd die! Why would you suggest such a thing?" To which the camel responded: "I just wanted to make the deal."

The audience roared. The story illustrates something that I'm sure they recognized. Financial-services salespeople can't just say anything to make the deal, but they do stretch it quite a bit. They are not true financial advisors—although the term financial advisor means virtually nothing in itself. You don't need any qualification to call yourself a financial advisor, as you do to be a Certified Financial Planner™ (CFP®) or a Registered Investment Advisor with the Securities and Exchange Commission (SEC).

The salespeople who work for the big brokerage houses, also known as wire houses, are required to bring in $10 million to $15 million a year. If they fall short, they get booted or their compensation gets reduced for the next year. The measure of their success is how much investment money they bring in. Very few firms, particularly in the wire house community, measure their people on the number of financial-planning engagements they set up. Those are time-consuming affairs, and they often are frowned upon.

Salespeople are not portfolio managers, and so they provide only minimal oversight. They don't want to get involved in comprehensive financial planning. Most are not trained in those complex areas and don't understand the issues. If such planning is offered at all, someone else in the firm provides it. The salesperson wants to move on to the next target.

THOSE LETTERS AFTER THE NAME

Those strings of letters that professionals put after their names often don't really stand for much. Others are highly significant: MD for medical doctor, for example; and, for lawyers, the JD of juris doctor. Those designations come with strict standards and testing.

In finance, the substantial credentials include CFA, or Chartered Financial Analyst®. This is a security analyst who works for a company that analyzes stocks and bonds and renders opinions. The designation is highly credentialed and requires a great deal of study. Sometimes CFAs have advisory clients, but generally they tend to be back-office people.

The CFP®, or Certified Financial Planner™, works more closely with consumers. This designation requires about two years of substantial study and testing. In the 1980s, when I went through the program, the certification required six independent tests in the areas of net worth, cash flow, time value of money, investments, insurance, taxes, retirement, and estate planning. The certification now requires at least two years of experience in the financial-services business along with passing a one-day, six-hour comprehensive exam.

You have no guarantee, however, that people who get that certification will be good at what they do. However, as CFP® licensees, they do have the education, training, and ethical obligation to provide quality service for their clients that should prepare them, if they choose to use their credentials well.

Anyone can call himself or herself a "financial advisor." The term in itself has little meaning, and it isn't regulated. Your pizza deliverer is free to give you financial advice. He can't deal in stocks and bonds on the exchange without a license, which requires a substantial amount of effort to acquire, and he can't charge a fee for financial advice unless he has state or federal registration, but he certainly can call himself a financial advisor. No regulation says he cannot.

Brokers who are licensed to sell stocks and bonds, however, do not necessarily know how to mix them effectively in a portfolio or how to effect the proper changes in a particular economic environment. The licensing means only that they demonstrated that they know the meaning of a stock, bond, mutual fund, etc. They understand enough to sell—they may gather assets, but that does not represent an ability to manage them.

When consumers see the CFP® designation, however, they have the reassurance that the advisor has gained a broad education in the financial matters needed to provide competent and comprehensive guidance. To become a registered investment advisor (RIA) with the Securities and Exchange Commission (SEC), anyone, including CFP® licensees need to have at least $100 million in assets under management. Those with assets less than $100 million must register with their respective state security agencies. Once registered, the advisor can charge a fee for services rather than collecting commissions on transactions.

When a CFP® licensee is an RIA, he or she is acting in the capacity of a *fiduciary*. That means the advisor has to put your best interest first, just as a doctor or lawyer or CPA must do. However, CFP® licensees who work for a major stock-brokerage company are not necessarily fiduciaries. They still could be asset gatherers. You have to ask the question: "Can you be a fiduciary if you are a commissioned stockbroker?" Possibly. But you will be better off if the manager of your investments is a CFP® professional and also an RIA who does not take commissions on transactions. That way, there is no conflict of interest. If an advisor is working as an RIA, he or she is a fiduciary under the Investment Advisers Act of 1940.

How do you know if your advisor is registered? You can visit the SEC website and look up advisors' names to see whether they are registered. The SEC also requires registered advisors to give you what is known as an ADV disclosure document that explains all the rules and stipulates that the advisor will be working on the client's behalf. It includes information on the advisor's education, fees, and strategies. **Registered investment advisors are in violation if they**

do not provide that document. If you are not given an ADV disclosure statement, you are not dealing with an SEC or state-registered advisor. You are dealing with a transaction broker.

The SEC recently has been pushing for regulations requiring advisors to be fiduciaries, and this has met considerable opposition from the big brokerage houses. They don't want their advisors to be fiduciaries. Why? Because it brings liability on the house. They know their brokers are asset gatherers. They are not money managers, and they're afraid to give them that responsibility. The fiduciary role could put them in legal jeopardy.

This is a matter of *caveat emptor*—"let the buyer beware." It's like going for a walk in the city: you can stroll through the best neighborhood in broad daylight, or you can venture down along the river at midnight. You're free to choose; nobody will stop you. Unfortunately, when it comes to financial issues, a lot of people don't know they're down by the river at midnight.

CHAPTER 5

IDENTIFYING THE RISKS

O ver the years, I have come across people who have engaged in what you might call peculiar investments. Some of those ideas were downright crazy. These were prospective clients who came to see me, and let me hasten to add that I did not participate in the schemes.

Two of the craziest that I recall were back in the 1980s, when people were looking for creative ways to overcome the high income tax rates. One was a tuna boat limited partnership. The gentleman saw a big opportunity. He experienced a big loss. Another would-be client spoke to me with wide eyes about cattle embryos. He had visions of getting rich on an investment that could be started in a petri dish. He had put down $10,000, just to get in on the action. He lost $10,000.

Everybody wants to find the next Microsoft or Apple or Amazon and get in at $2 a share and watch it grow to $1,000. Those bonanzas are so rare that they're not worth chasing. Finding that winner probably will mean losing on many others. Not everyone is a Peter Lynch, the legendary fund manager who searched for "ten-bagger" investments with the potential for explosive growth. If you think that you or your advisor can do that, good luck, but the strategy is highly unlikely to be productive. It's like a dog chasing its tail. Not to diminish his enormous skills, but Peter Lynch managed money in the greatest bull market in history, 1982–2000.

On any given day, only a handful of stocks drive up the averages on the indexes. Research shows that perhaps a third of the top one hundred stocks will drive a day's entire return. In fact, the other two thirds typically lose value, but the positive ones do so well that they pull up the average for the whole group. What this means is that a stock picker has a 33 percent chance of success. That's hardly a good deal.

Now of course you're not throwing darts to pick stocks. Good managers will know where to look to increase the chances of success, but the reality is that 85 percent of mutual-fund managers do not beat their own benchmark index. Why? The fees within mutual funds are part of the reason, but that statistic highlights the difficulty of consistently picking winners.

That's the nature of investment risk, which for most people is what comes to mind first when they consider what might threaten their wealth. The market, however, is only one of many risks. Inflation, for example, erodes purchasing power over the years. It has been decades since inflation ran rampant, but people of retirement age have not forgotten those years, and it remains a major concern, even at normal rates. Taxation, if improperly managed, also can reduce returns excessively and dilute the financial legacy for the next generation. And as people live longer, not only must their savings serve them for many years, but they also increasingly face the prospect of needing expensive long-term care.

Risk management is a key element of comprehensive financial planning. If you prepare properly, you can manage all of those threats effectively so that they do not destroy your retirement dreams. In this chapter, we will take a closer look at some of those risks, including investment concerns. I have devoted separate chapters to two risks in particular: taxation and long-term care.

DEALING WITH MARKET RISK

In the stock market, you basically can face three types of risk: market risk, sector risk, and individual risk. These are important factors to consider when deciding the manner in which to buy and sell equities.

Market risk is inherent, whether you are buying an individual stock, a mutual fund, or an exchange-traded fund (ETF). As the market goes, so go portfolios. Your investments are likely to have some correlation to the broad indexes.

What can you do about that? You can diversify into different types of equity. One approach is to buy a mutual fund or ETF that has a variety of stocks within it. An assortment of financial instruments in your portfolio can go far in reducing market risk.

You are facing sector risk if your investments include a concentration of the stock of companies in a particular industry, such as technology or utilities or health care. These are companies that provide the same or a related product or service, such as pharmaceutical manufacturers. At any given time, the business cycle may or may not favor a sector. Things beyond your control—societal trends, government policy, world events—will smile or frown upon a particular industry. If that entire industry should start to slip in the market, whatever portion of your portfolio is invested in it will follow suit. When the Federal Reserve raises interest rates, for example, utilities tend to slip because they operate in an environment that involves a lot of borrowing. Your particular investment might not fall as much as others, or it might fall more—either way, you can expect to get caught up in the sector risk, regardless of what company you may own in that sector.

Individual risk is what you face when you hold any stock. On any given trading day, it is likely that at least two individual stocks among the nearly three thousand companies that trade on the New York Stock Exchange will drop by 20 percent or more. In 2015, for example, many stocks declined in price by 50 percent or more, even though the NYSE as a whole dropped no more than 10 percent in August.

If you hold that stock, your value declines. If you keep holding it, your value declines more if the stock sinks more. If you are not diversified, your portfolio's fortunes will rise and fall on that company's performance. Along with that individual stock risk, you face both the market risk and the sector risk as well. All three factors work in concert.

Clearly, the way to diminish those risks is to design a portfolio that is well diversified among asset classes and sectors. Once done, however, that portfolio will need to be regularly monitored. As time goes by, the asset classes and sectors that have done well will claim a larger percentage of your overall portfolio. That happens naturally as your winning stocks grow in proportion and your losing ones represent a smaller percentage of your holdings.

This calls for regular monitoring to make sure that your overall portfolio remains aligned with the risk tolerance that you originally set forth in your financial planning. The discipline of rebalancing is essential in that regard. When you rebalance, you shave gains off of positions that are up, and you put that money into some of the positions that temporarily are down, presuming you still want them. That way you are locking in profits, buying at a bargain, and keeping your risk level right where you want it.

Some investors rebalance quarterly, but I believe rebalancing should take place when there are market corrections, which happen once or twice a year. That way, the positions can run a little longer—and the ones that keep running tend to be those that are heading into positive territory. Why take them off the track quite so soon? Nothing runs forever, however, and that trend is bound to reverse. When it does, it's time to rebalance. Of course, that requires that someone be watching. That someone will need the training and experience to recognize what is happening and when to act [See page 74–75].

Most salespeople will put people's assets into mutual funds with managers who do not actively buy and sell. An active manager searches for positive positions and will sell to protect assets during corrections and bear markets. Few managers operate that way, and that is why we have that general statistic that only 15 percent of them outperform their benchmark indexes. Most mutual-fund managers have a mandate to invest according to their index. For example, the S&P 500 might be the "bogey," the industry term for a performance benchmark. The manager will trade equities to reflect the weighting of the stocks represented in the S&P 500 index. Since the manager is measured by the benchmark, he or she doesn't stray from it and will aim to build the same percentages into the fund.

In doing so, however, the fund will incur transaction costs, and how does that serve the investor? You can buy an exchange-traded fund of the S&P 500 for a few tenths of a percent a year in expenses, which is about as close to free as you can get. Why would you instead pay 1 percent or more? The mutual-fund company claims those high, built-in costs at four o'clock p.m. every day before quoting the net asset value (NAV). That's the net after fees and expenses, which can be 1 or 2 percent. It's a cost you do not see. A competent advisor knows which fund managers earn their fee, depending upon their performance relative to their benchmark.

Those fees and expenses also have much to do with why mutual-fund managers have a difficult time beating their benchmarks. When they are investing that close to the benchmark, they can't possibly outperform. Some managers will separate from the benchmark during a downturn, actively trying to protect assets. A good advisor will seek out such managers.

ETFs have become more popular in difficult periods such as the years following the turn of the millennium. The annual expenses of ETFs can be a fraction of the costs incurred in mutual funds. ETFs are built like a mutual fund but traded like a stock, which also presents an advantage to advisors who know what they are doing. My point, though, is not that you want to do a lot of trading. My point is that the expenses are remarkably low. Also, unlike mutual funds, ETFs do not distribute capital gains in December. Because they trade like stocks, they are similar to stocks in that they only distribute capital gains when the position is sold. **This is a major consideration for taxable accounts of high-net-worth individuals.**

ETFs, however, are not actively managed. They are generally composed of securities that mirror a distinct index. For example, the index might be the top S&P companies or the Dow 30 or the six hundred small-cap stocks. It could be an index of international equities, utilities, or Treasury bonds. That's why the expenses are low: the funds are not managed. That's all right, but only if you or your advisor is watching over your investment, making sure that it is performing as it should. The need for that oversight is the central theme of this book.

For high-income people, ETFs are a better way to invest. ETFs offer more diversification. If, for example, you believe that biotechnology is the wave of the future, you can select an ETF for that sector. That way you get a cross-section of biotech companies, rather than trying to gamble on the one you think might introduce the next super drug, which could turn out to be a flop. You might feel like taking a shot on some small biotech firm, but beware: you might lose everything you put into it. It is often better to buy a biotech ETF and get an assortment of the established and proven firms as well as some smaller ones, depending upon the fund. Biotech companies, however, are high-risk offerings, and they and their ETFs should be treated accordingly.

PURCHASING POWER RISK

If I were to point to a single risk that is the number-one problem in retirement, it would be the loss of purchasing power over the years as inflation nibbles away at the value of portfolios. Fifty years ago, a postage stamp cost a nickel. Gasoline was about thirty cents a gallon, and a gallon of milk cost less than a dollar. Compare those prices with what you pay today, and you have a clear picture of the effects of inflation over half a century.

Even at so-called normal inflation rates, the loss of purchasing power will be significant over the two or three decades of a typical retirement. It is normal, and you can expect it. So how do you figure out how much it will cut into your buying power?

Let's go back to that *Rule of Seventy-Two*, the formula for determining how long it will take invested money to double at any given rate of return. If you divide seventy-two by that rate, you get the length of time. The formula also can be used to calculate how long it will take, at a given inflation rate, for the cost of things to double. Let's say that the inflation rate moving forward will average about 3 percent, which has been typical in the decades since the government began tracking it. If you divide seventy-two by three, the answer is twenty-four years.

That means those entering retirement in 2016 can expect that in 2040, they will be paying twice as much, on average, as they do now for consumer goods and services. With today's longevity and quality of health care, many will still be living active lives in their eighties, but they will need twice as much income then. In other words, even if their portfolio value stayed exactly the same, it in effect would be worth half as much. A retiree who is spending $50,000 a year currently for living expenses will need to spend $100,000 a year just to maintain the same standard of living. This is the where the phrase "living on fixed income" gets its ugly meaning.

That loss of purchasing power is a highly significant consideration, and yet it tends not to loom large in people's minds as they plan for their retirement. A good advisor will build that inflation risk into the cash-flow model so that the investments keep pace with the inflation rate. Think about what is happening as you withdraw from your portfolio: if you take out a typical 4 percent annually for living expenses, inflation is silently slipping out an additional 3 percent. You therefore need a 7 percent return on your investments to break even.

In the eighties and nineties, that was relatively easy to accomplish. Since 2000, it has been very difficult. In fact, most people who have been taking out 4 percent from their portfolio since 2000 actually now have less than when they started. Those losses in the first three years of the millennium, and later in 2008, delivered a devastating blow. Those whose portfolios were handled properly didn't lose as much, but many were on autopilot and risked that headlong dive.

Even in this climate of relatively low returns, inflation is still at work, and though it has been relatively low, it is bound to return to historic averages. To compensate, a lot of people have been increasing the risk in their portfolios, but again, that requires the counsel of a competent advisor with the sell discipline to protect the portfolio in a down period. That's not an easy task for a competent advisor, let alone self-directed investors who manage their own money.

Whether you call it inflation risk or purchasing-power risk, it is the single most significant issue facing retirees trying to make the most of their portfolios. Inflation, along with taxes and fees, must always be kept top of mind as you strive to get a reasonable return that won't let you down.

INTEREST-RATE RISK

If you are retired or nearing retirement age, you certainly remember those days of decades past when even a simple bank investment could command a decent interest rate. Of course, those were also the days of the WIN buttons, when "Whip Inflation Now" was a catchphrase of the Gerald Ford administration, so investors certainly needed those high interest rates to keep up.

Nonetheless, people looked at the return they could get on a certificate of deposit, and they felt a sense of reassurance that their savings would see them through. For a time, the return on some CDs was nearly 16 percent. A retiree could put a modest life savings of, say, $300,000 in such a CD for an income of $48,000 a year. Add to that a Social Security benefit and a pension, and it might have seemed a dream retirement.

The trouble comes when those CDs mature, but it's time to reinvest, and those rates have vanished. Today, an investment of that size might bring in, at best, a paltry $3,000, and that would be for a five-year CD. Several years ago, you could get a 4 or 5 percent return. And there you have the essence of interest-rate risk: people who pin their retirement hopes on the interest rates of the moment could be in for an unhappy surprise if those rates sink. By the time that taxes and inflation claim their share, the net return could be less than zero—and that, of course, is deadly to a portfolio and a person's standard of living . . .

Most commonly, the concept of interest-rate risk is applied to bond investments. As I pointed out earlier, bond investors ride a seesaw: as interest rates rise, the value of existing bonds naturally falls as investors look for a better opportunity somewhere else. It's only when rates are falling that a higher-yielding bond becomes increasingly attractive.

A LONG WAY TO GO

Sometimes people get the impression that when they flip that switch to enter retirement, they have to stop taking risk. It is simply not true. Most people will have miles to go before they sleep, and they will need money to pay for all those years of living that are still to come. The government's withdrawal table for IRAs goes all the way to age 115. As life expectancy continues to increase, the impact on personal financial planning will be huge.

That longevity means you still need investment growth because, as we have seen, market risk is not the only threat you face. You need a portfolio with a portion of equities, and if you invest in bonds, they need to be the appropriate type for the current environment. That's yet one more reason you need an advisor who cares enough about you to guide you in the right direction, keeping a close watch on the trends.

CHAPTER 6

TAX INTELLIGENCE

When Ronald Reagan still was making films in the early 1960s, he was reluctant to do another shoot if it was near the end of the year. To him, it meant he would do all that work just to see the IRS stake a 90 percent claim on his additional income—so why bother?

In those days, that was the highest marginal tax rate. And it was a shame, as he stated, because forgoing a movie also meant no work for the one hundred or so people on the crew. Reagan saw the progressive tax rate as a fundamental flaw in our system—one that stifles productivity and innovation. And that is why reducing those high marginal rates was a goal for his administration when he became president.

He wasn't the first to take such action. The marginal tax rates also were reduced under the administration of President John F. Kennedy, stimulating a boom in the economy. They called those years the go-go sixties. And then along came President Lyndon Johnson and his Great Society. The rising taxes in the ensuing years contributed to recession and stagnant growth in the 1970s. StockCharts data indicates that during the period of 1966 to 1982, the Dow Jones Industrial Average gained 5 percent, cumulative. Not per year—the total gain was only 5 percent in all those years . . . essentially flat.

Taxes clearly play a critical role in the productivity and growth of our society. When Reagan lowered the marginal rates, the economy exploded in 1982, and when President Bill Clinton lowered rates in the 1990s, the momentum in the economy and stock market continued. After President George W. Bush lowered some rates in the 2000s, the economy grew until 2008.

The lowering of marginal rates consistently has helped the economy—despite the bear markets we have encountered for other reasons. The prevailing rates have not been a matter of which party is in power, as two of those presidents who reduced them were Democrats, and two were Republicans. Some will proclaim otherwise, but as Daniel Patrick Moynihan, former speaker of the House, famously said: "Everyone is entitled to his own opinion but not to his own facts."

Some people hold fast to the ridiculous notion that the wealthy do not pay their fair share of taxes. They chant that mantra so often that many come to accept it as fact, but it's far from the truth. The fact is that the wealthiest 1 percent of the population pay about 39 percent of the taxes in this country. The top 5 percent pay about 55 percent of the total taxes. The top 10 percent pay about 75 percent. And about half of the people in this country pay no taxes at all. The opinions do not match the facts, but because the public is unaware of the truth, such distortions can be perpetuated.

I point this out not to discount the wisdom of our progressive tax system, and I do not know any people of high net worth who feel they should not pay taxes. Still, after paying the bulk of the taxes in this country, the wealthy certainly should not be demonized. They are carrying much of the tax burden and should not be dragged through the dirt and accused of dodging a responsibility that they take quite seriously.

I often tell my clients that the fact that they owe taxes is a good sign because it means they made money. If you don't pay taxes, it means you didn't make money. That's not a good thing. What *is* a good thing is to understand how the IRS code offers incentives that can reduce taxes. You should not be paying more taxes than necessary, and a great many people do just that.

Everything is relative, and that is certainly true with taxes. If you're making $20,000 a year, you don't pay much in taxes. But if you are married and filing jointly, making $466,950 in 2016, as a lot of dual-earning-household corporate executives and professionals do, you will be hitting that top tax rate—currently at 39.6 percent with an additional 3.4 percent for the Obamacare surcharge. And then there is the 7.65 percent for Social Security (US Tax Code 2015). And let's not forget state taxes, sales taxes, gasoline taxes, and all the others.

High-net-worth people lose, on average, more than half their money to taxation, and that's a fact that a lot of people want to ignore. It must not be a fact that a financial advisor ignores, however, because the savings in taxes can be significant. Some people believe tax-deferred annuities are an answer, but they are *not*—for many reasons that we will examine in chapter 8.

TAX-LOSS HARVESTING

Tax-loss harvesting is where advisors can really earn their stripes. This is the strategy of selling (at a loss) a position (shares of security you own) in your portfolio that may temporarily be in the negative and then buying a similar position to balance the portfolio and create an opportunity for a legitimate tax write-off. In other words, by moving from one security to another in that manner, you will be showing, on paper, a capital loss.

Let's say you have a stock or an ETF or a mutual fund that has fallen below its cost basis, which can happen in a market correction. You can sell it and write off the loss. If you truly like that security, you can buy back into it after thirty days, thus avoiding what is known as the wash-sale rule, an IRS regulation that would otherwise disallow the deduction.

This requires close monitoring of your portfolio because the harvesting must be done whenever the opportunity appears, such as in a market decline. That might be in May or in August. If you wait until December, those temporary losses will be gone. An advisor who is knowledgeable and vigilant will understand how to do this properly. Through annual tax harvesting, you can knock out most of the capital gains in a portfolio—and a million-dollar portfolio might have $40,000 in capital gains. By eliminating those gains, you also are eliminating the 20 percent tax on them. That's $8,000 saved, simply by carefully repositioning the portfolio at the right time. Self-directed investors might wish to take note of this example of how knowledgeable advisors can earn their fees in many ways besides performance.

The focus of such a strategy, of course, is your taxable accounts. There are no tax-loss harvesting opportunities in a tax-deferred account, such as an IRA or 401(k), in which you get total tax deferral until you withdraw it as ordinary income. Mutual funds are not tax efficient in any year because by statute, they must distribute both dividends and capital gains at year-end, regardless of performance gain in that calendar year. A mutual fund, even if it shows an overall loss for the year, can create a large capital-gains obligation in

December because of all the trading conducted within it throughout the year. That isn't a problem in an IRA, but it can be a big problem in a taxable account.

TAX DEFERRAL PROS AND CONS

A major mistake that many people make is to invest their entire life savings in an IRA or 401(k)-type plan. Saving money of course is a good idea—you need to store that flour somewhere if you're going to make bread—but you must consider the tax implications.

First of all, if most all of your money is in a tax-deferred account, you will be losing at least a quarter of it to taxation when you begin taking it out during retirement. If all of your money is in such a retirement plan, you will need about 25 percent more because of those income taxes that you deferred for years but that now will be due.

Some of your money therefore should be in a taxable account that is properly managed with tax-loss harvesting and other investment strategies. If you balance your savings between a taxable account and a deferred account, you can avoid getting waffled by taxes when you begin those withdrawals. Portfolio withdrawals during retirement can occur for as many years as it took to get that money in.

Nonetheless, 401(k) plans and IRAs are a good idea overall, despite the tax hit when the money comes out. Most people should invest in them. That tax deferral gives you a powerful advantage. You're getting what amounts to free money up front from the deduction and possibly from a company match.

Among the many considerations of tax-deferred retirement plans is the fact that upon reaching age seventy and a half, you will be required to begin the annual withdrawals, known as required minimum distributions (RMDs), which get larger as the years go by.

If perchance you should skip one, you will be charged a penalty of 50 percent of the amount that you were supposed to take out—not a good idea.

This calls for careful management. You are of course responsible for your own tax liabilities, though the custodians of the IRA or pension plan normally help with this issue. Your advisor can also help you understand and assist with this tax-sensitive requirement. The withdrawal can get complicated if you have more than one qualified account because the RMD is figured in aggregate. You can spread it out among the accounts. It is likely that you will want help with that because inadvertently getting the math wrong could expose you to a big penalty. The easiest path is to let each custodian withdraw the RMD amounts from the accounts they have in their custody. Ultimately, the taxpayer is responsible for the proper withdrawal amounts annually.

A nice provision of an IRA is that your heirs have the option, if the documentation is set up properly, of continuing the tax deferral, stretching it out over *their* lifetimes. That is sometimes called a *stretch* IRA, although that does not mean it is some special type of IRA account. The term simply is pointing out the provision of the IRS code that allows the beneficiary, such as a child, to receive the money over a lifetime.

When a spouse is the beneficiary, it's a different matter: the spouse can simply keep the plan going as it was, making withdrawals as needed, or roll it into his or her own IRA. Anyone else who inherits the money, though, must withdraw it, either as a lump sum with all the tax due at once; in installments with taxes due over five years; or as a stretch, taking withdrawals as RMDs during the course of his or her lifetime. To do the stretch, however, the heir must begin taking the annual RMD over his or her life expectancy beginning no later than December 31 of the year following the original account holder's death. Failure to do so is a mistake that often foils the opportunity. CPAs and good tax advisors know the rules and can make sure it's all set up properly.

CONVERTING TO A ROTH

Another effective way to manage taxes is to convert a traditional IRA into a tax-free Roth IRA. It can make sense to do so after retirement, when your income levels are lower and you can withdraw money from your traditional plan without penalty. Of course, you have to pay the tax on the IRA conversion, but that works out to be a good deal for some people. If you have a high net worth and do not need to use your IRA money, it is likely that you will be passing it on to your heirs—and somebody will be paying income tax at some point. Either you will pay the taxes as you withdraw money while you are alive, or they will pay the taxes after they inherit it. The longer the account grows, the more the taxes will be.

If you and your advisor determine that a Roth conversion is a good strategy for you, you can start transferring money in increments. It is important to manage those withdrawals every year so that you do not end up in a higher bracket. Your aim is to keep your tax to a minimum. Meanwhile, as the money builds inside the Roth, it continues to grow—but it does so free of taxes after an initial five-year period that starts with the first year contribution. Whoever withdraws it someday, whether that is you or your heirs, will not need to pay income tax. I have never seen retirees actually use that money themselves. It goes to their heirs, who can get it as a lump sum without pushing their tax brackets sky high. The money is subject to estate tax, however—but that's another issue.

If you need the money for living expenses, it makes no sense to convert to a Roth. In other words, the proper strategy will depend upon your situation, which you and your advisor will need to examine. There are no blanket rules.

SO MUCH TO CONSIDER

In this chapter, we have taken a look primarily at income taxes and capital-gains taxes and some of the tools and strategies you can use to manage them effectively. We have not, however, covered the spectrum of tax issues that are involved in comprehensive financial planning. It is estimated that the tax code is seventy-seven thousand pages in length. No one person can know it all. Depending upon the complexity of an estate, three advisors should be working together: the CFP® licensee, a CPA, and perhaps a tax attorney.

There is so much to consider on this topic of taxation. For example, a Roth IRA is income tax-free but not estate tax-free. This also applies to municipal bonds and life insurance proceeds. The management of federal estate taxes and state inheritance taxes plays a significant role when it comes to efficiently arranging a financial legacy for the next generation and generations beyond.

The whole area of tax planning should be void of emotion. Lacking good advice, an investor might hesitate to sell a position that has made a lot of money in a lengthy bull market, shuddering at the thought of paying so much in capital-gains tax. So he holds tight, and along comes the bear. He ends up losing far more of his position than the tax would have claimed. In response, he digs in, determined to hold on even longer. "It'll come back," he tries to tell himself. Maybe, or maybe not. If it does, it could take years. Either way, it makes no sense to let the tax decision control the investment decision. It's the tail wagging the dog.

The issues of financial planning overlap and interrelate, and each must be examined in the context of the others. An all-encompassing plan will ensure that all the elements of your financial life work together so that your money will last and serve you well. Tax management is one of those elements that must not be overlooked. That is why you are finding references to taxes in virtually every chapter of this book. And that is why I keep coming back to this central point: if you hope to do this right, you need to be working with an advisor who possesses a level of sophistication to help you make the right choices.

CHAPTER 7

AFFORDING LONG-TERM CARE

As people live ever longer, the prospect that at some point they will need long-term care comes increasingly to the forefront. It is a medical issue, of course, brought on by years of those wondrous advances in the health field, but it is also a financial issue. In short: it's expensive, and it's a clear risk to the portfolio.

As we age, physical ailments are part of the program. We all know that, and most people accept it. You might be thankful for the medical knowledge that has prolonged life, but in doing so, it also has presented new issues related to that longevity. Do we really want to live to one hundred and beyond if we are in pain and we cannot take care of ourselves?

The need for long-term care has become a huge issue, and it is not going to go away. It's far from inevitable, though. I have seen most of my clients live well into their eighties and nineties without needing such care. Most of the couples with whom I have worked do take care of themselves, and if one takes ill, the other willingly steps forward to be the caregiver.

But who will take care of the survivor? Will it be one of the children? If a parent needs round-the-clock care, is it fair to expect someone in the family to provide it? It can be an onerous responsibility, both physically and emotionally.

To commingle health with finances is a difficult marriage. The subject elicits all manner of anxieties and emotions within a family. Retirees may somehow feel that spending their money just to take care of themselves is somehow squandering their life's work—or at least they regret the need to set aside their best-laid plans and retirement dreams to pay those bills. Meanwhile the children, though they would seldom say so outright, see their inheritance being used up to take care of their parents and wonder how long this might go on. Sometimes I am appalled by the attitudes. But I also understand the point.

Long-term care planning is an important aspect of preparing for retirement, and there are proper ways to approach this contingency that many families experience. None of those proper options involve giving up all your money just to avoid the possibility that you might have to use it for long-term care. Let's take a look at the ways in which many people approach the management of this risk.

COVERING YOUR RISK

You can buy an insurance policy to cover expenses associated with extended care. If you choose to do so, you should buy the insurance while you still are healthy, preferably in your fifties or earlier. The declination rate is high: insurers are cautious about whom they will cover, and those who have already demonstrated that they are most likely to make use of a policy will be least likely to get one. A heart attack, major illness, back surgery, joint replacement—with multiple conditions such as these, you can count yourself out of the running for long-term care (LTC) insurance coverage.

A straight-up LTC policy tends to be expensive. That is because a few decades ago, when they were introduced, the insurance companies lacked the experience of aggregate claims. They didn't really know what they were getting into. Now that they see how high the claims have become, the premiums have doubled. For a lot of people, traditional LTC insurance is becoming unaffordable. It's less expensive when you are in your forties and fifties. If you wait until your sixties, you will be paying $3,000 or $4,000 a year per person depending on the coverage selected.

In recent years, people have also had the option of purchasing investment products or life insurance policies that include riders for long-term care. New products have been coming out that will provide varying degrees of coverage for the care in the event that it becomes necessary. Those who never need the care will still get some benefit from their investments. If it is a life insurance policy, for example, a payout would still go to the beneficiary. Such features are designed to address people's oft-expressed concern about paying expensive premiums for years on a traditional LTC policy that they might never need.

Some of the new LTC plans allow a one-time payment or periodic payments into an investment account: $50,000, for example, might pay out $200,000 in LTC benefits depending on the participant's age when he or she started the plan. If some or all of the benefits are never used for long-term care, a named beneficiary receives the original investment (or more) when the insured dies.

The new investment-style LTC policies have no minimum time associated with the withdrawals, only the annual amount of money available to withdraw from the plan. Remember, insurance is passing some of the risk to someone else, the insurance company.

Other people simply choose to self-insure, and that is an option for people of high net worth. If you have $5 million or $10 million, for example, self-insuring could make sense for you. At that level of wealth, you stand a good chance of being able to afford the costs, which average about $75,000 a year in 2016 dollars. As the population ages and demand for long-term care services increases, however, that figure likely will be rising annually at a faster pace than the overall inflation rate. Your Social Security benefit could help to cover some of that cost, but the expense is still daunting.

If you or your spouse should happen to need help, you may not necessarily need a level of care that requires admission to a facility providing 24/7 monitoring. Many people will need less expensive custodial or intermediate care, in which they get help with dressing, bathing, perhaps taking medications, either in a LTC facility or at home. LTC policies typically cover home-care expenses. Much of that care can be provided adequately by someone without medical, nursing, or other professional training. The new LTC policies cover that expense as well.

Increasingly popular are senior facilities with assisted-living options in which residents have their own condominium or apartment. They can enter such facilities while they are still healthy and can care for themselves. If they wish, they can dine daily in a common area with others in the community rather than prepare their own meals. If the status of their health eventually changes, they can take advantage of the more advanced services and professional staffing that many of these facilities offer. The residents can move on to intermediate care and then to extended or long-term care.

Another possibility is to make arrangements with someone in your family to become your caregiver—but that option, too, calls for great caution. You must not presume that your daughter or son will be able to handle that responsibility. Your children likely have jobs and families of their own, and as much as they love you, that duty could become a heavy burden on them. Depression is common among caregivers. If you're just getting a bit forgetful, your children certainly can be a big help. But if you require constant care, it is unlikely that they will be able to provide what you need. Caring for an older person, even a loved one, is not the same as caring for an infant or a child when life issues were simpler. It is sometimes an overload for the caregiver, as the complications of their own health and family issues collide with those of the parent.

DON'T GIVE YOUR MONEY AWAY

Faced with the prospect that they might have to pay a fortune for long-term care, some people decide that to protect their life savings, they will just give all their money to their children so that they qualify for Medicaid coverage. To qualify for government assistance, you first must spend down your own assets.

If that is a strategy that you intend to pursue, understand that if you do enter a facility, the state will be examining your finances for the previous five years. This is called the look-back period. If the state determines that you have transferred assets in that period, you will be disqualified.

There are moral issues involved in the strategy, however. If you have money, why should the taxpayers be paying for you? I regularly ask clients to consider that question. And beyond those ethical considerations, you need to ask yourself whether you will be getting the quality of care that you would want in such a situation. Nursing homes have few beds for Medicaid patients due to the lower reimbursement considerations.

In any event, you must be very careful about giving your money away. I recall a case years ago in Trenton, NJ, in which a widow put the deed to her house and all of her bank accounts in her daughter's name. Her daughter and son-in-law were living with her, but a few years later they divorced. The husband got control of the house—and kicked the woman out of her own home.

The lesson there is that if you are going to retitle your assets to your children, you might want to use a trust. Morally, however, I do not believe you should do that for the purpose of receiving state assistance. The risk that you face might not be as great as you imagine. Insurance industry statistics suggest the average stay in a nursing home is only two years, and it's that long only because of the longevity of Alzheimer's patients.

CHAPTER 8

KEEPING THE CASH FLOWING

Positive cash flow is just a fancy accounting term that means more money is coming in than expenses are going out. Most people can understand that simple concept, even if the government does not. Of course, the government, with its $19 trillion national debt, can borrow a lot of money and not have to pay it back. The rest of us don't have that luxury.

In the accumulation stage of your life, positive cash flow means that your salary is providing you enough money so that you can set some of it aside as retirement savings, either in a taxable account or in a deferred tax plan such as a 401(k) or IRA.

When you are in your retirement years, the table turns. No longer are you working to produce that positive cash flow. Now, you are depending upon your savings to do that work for you. Often, people begin to struggle because those savings are insufficient to do the job. They cannot sustain the lifestyle to which they have been accustomed during their working years. Much of the time, the root of the problem has been a lack of planning. Only 28 percent—a figure derived from the cumulative results of multiple national surveys—of people believe they have enough money to sustain their retirement years.

WHY GIVE IT ALL AWAY?

In my three decades in this industry, I have been puzzled time and again by people's willingness to give away their money in exchange for a guarantee. It's a question for the academics who study behavioral finance: Why in the world do people do such a thing?

My number-one rule of retirement income planning is to not give up your principal to an insurance company. And yet that is what countless people have unwittingly done, often as a result of unethical or misleading sales practices.

Typically, when people retire on a defined-benefit pension plan, they have several standard options. They can accept, for example, the *life only* option of perhaps $2,000 a month, and when they die, their spouse gets nothing. Not too many people like that option, so other choices are a *joint and survivor* 50 percent payout to the spouse, or 75 percent, or the option of continuing the full benefit.

However, there's a catch to all those options, and that is a reduction in the monthly amount received up front. That $2,000, for example, could become $1,800 a month for the 50 percent option, or $1,600 a month to retain the full payment to a spouse. In other words, you lose part of your income on a monthly basis (for life) in exchange for a guarantee at some later point.

What are you doing when you accept those options? You're buying an insurance policy. To give up $400 a month means you are in effect spending $4,800 a year, or $48,000 over ten years, or $96,000 over twenty years for life insurance. That's a lot of money, and for some reason, namely to get that guarantee, people will do this. They are averse to risk. For emotional reasons, that is under-standable. From a financial point of view, it makes no sense.

What, then, might you do instead? About twenty years ago, following a challenge from IBM, another option was permitted in the pension regulations, and that is the lump-sum payout. In other words, the pension plan says: "Here's a pile of money instead of a monthly payment, so take it and leave us alone."

In response, a lot of people still choose that monthly guaran-teed check rather than the lump sum of money, which might be hundreds of thousands of dollars. If you do that, you are giving up that sum to an insurance company. When you and your spouse have died, nobody will be getting anything. The insurance company gets to keep the principal.

On their part, the insurance companies no doubt would argue that they are taking on the risk. And that is true. They are correct. But their actuaries have figured out the statistics and probabilities of who will be dying and when, and you can be sure that the insurance companies have left themselves plenty of room to make a lot of money, which is perfectly normal in our free-market environment.

Suppose I were to say to a wealthy client, "How about if you give me all your money and I'll guarantee you 6 percent for the rest of your life, but whenever you die I get to keep all that money. Is that okay with you?" I daresay the response would be a double take and a resounding "no!" And yet so many people are willing to give such a deal to an insurance company.

Sure, it's nice to get a monthly check. Your Social Security benefit comes monthly, too, and that's nice. But in exchange for that monthly pension check, you are giving up the flexibility that a lump sum could provide you. It's yours to use as you wish, or invest, or leave to your children. You could buy a car or go on vacation if you wanted. "No," you might say, "I can't use that principal!" But that's what the insurance company is doing. It's taking your principal, using it to buy Treasury bonds, covering its expenses with it, and giving you back a little along the way. You could do the same, for that matter, and you would be keeping your money to leave to the kids someday, or to charity.

INVESTING FOR CASH FLOW

My suggestion for retirement security is to have faith in the economy and invest your savings in good companies. You will make money over time—not every year, but most years. Done wisely, with good guidance, your wins will outpace your losses over time. That's your best bet for producing the positive cash flow of a thriving retirement. That's the wise way to replace your paycheck, not with some guarantee from an insurance company. If you consume some of the principal in off-market cycles, so what? It is your money to use for as long as you live.

In the first decade of retirement, you do need to be careful about spending down your principal. After that first decade, it is unlikely that you will be doing as much world traveling or playing as much golf. There's always the exception: the Uncle Ernie who golfs into his nineties and the neighbor Sally who plays tennis at ninety-five. But the reality is that most people slow down. In my observation, people over seventy-five are less active and spend less money. What that also means is that spending some of your principal after that age is not such a big deal. Unless you plan to buy a Ferrari, you're not going to run out of money. You can't be foolish, but I haven't seen that very often.

To help cover the risk of spending down principal in that first ten years, some people employ the concept of pension maximization. If you are getting a lump sum at retirement, you might wish to buy an insurance policy that would pay that amount if you were to die during that time. That would be expensive over the course of an entire retirement, particularly if you wanted that coverage in your eighties and nineties, but you're really just looking for protection during that first decade. After that, you and your surviving spouse are not facing as much risk if you are spending down principal.

Let's face it: you essentially are buying an insurance policy anyway when you accept a lower monthly pension payment in return for that guarantee that your spouse will continue to get something if you die first. You can find a way to manage that risk yourself. It amazes me that people are so willing to give up hundreds of thousands of dollars for some bogus guarantee. It's legal, of course, but from a financial point of view, it is questionable. If your spouse dies first, the built-in insurance payment of a joint-and-survivor reduced monthly payment continues. Your option decision cannot be reversed.

I find it ironic that the same people who are willing to give their money to an insurance company are the same ones who balk at the thought of stocks in their portfolio. "It's too risky! I can't afford to lose money in retirement!" they say . . . so why, then, can they afford to give it away?

This is an issue of behavioral finance. It gets back to the balance of greed and fear, and this is the fear aspect that is rearing up. This is where they are telling Monty Hall that they will just accept the thousand dollars, thank you, and never mind what's behind those three doors. It might feel like the comfortable and safe way to go, but when it comes to their retirement, that attitude can be financially dissatisfying for a lot of people.

THE ANNUITY TRAP

Buying an annuity to quell those fears puts you in the same type of situation with an insurance company as you face when making a pension decision. Salespeople spend countless TV hours hawking the notion of a guaranteed retirement income, with no stocks and bonds involved. What do you think they are selling? They are selling annuities. Annuities are massively marketed, and they are one of the most oversold and manipulated legal sales products in the financial-services industry.

The word "annuity" is actually just an accounting term for a string of payments over a period of time. It is not an insurance product, but the insurance industry has hijacked the word. You give your money to the insurance company, and in return, you get a string of payments for a period of time—ten years, for example, or for life—just as you would receive with a pension. When you die, with few exceptions, your heirs get nothing.

Essentially that is the same as when you choose a monthly pension payment option rather than taking the lump sum. You begin getting that monthly pension payment because your company has purchased an annuity with an insurance company.

Let's say you won't be getting a pension. One day you get a flashy invitation to a seminar at a restaurant. There you hear a speaker waxing eloquent about how you can get a guaranteed income for life, while a team of salespeople wait to hover over you. The reason I find that to be disturbing is that many of the attendees at those seminars lack the financial sophistication to know what they are doing. Annuities are one of the more complicated and complex financial instruments known to man. When you get that eighty-page color brochure, you easily can become dazzled and confused to the point where you lose sight of what is going on.

Here's what is going on. The essence of the deal is a statement that amounts to something like this: "We will give you a 6 percent guarantee when you annuitize your contract." Unfortunately, few people understand what annuitization means. It means you give up your principal to an insurance company. In return, the company will provide that string of payments. That's what you get. What the salespeople get is a commission of 5 to 8 percent. By working a crowded seminar room of twenty or thirty people or more, they can rake in $50,000 to $100,000 in a single night.

Yes, it's legal. But is it ethical? Let's take a closer look at that 6 percent guarantee. These are not fixed annuities. A fixed annuity is an insurance company's equivalent of a bank CD and, depending upon the level of US Treasury interest rates, might pay only 1 or 2 percent annually. An indexed annuity, for example, uses expensive covered-call options to finance the product and offers perhaps 1 percent above CD rates. You don't necessarily have to give up your principal, but you're not going to make much money, and you will be paying income tax on it at your marginal rate (not good for high-net-worth couples). When an insurance company offers you a guarantee such as 6 percent, however, that product actually is an annuity that is investing in stocks and bonds, a variable annuity. If the company is paying you 6 percent, it would need to make perhaps 10 percent to cover your 6 percent payment and its average 4 percent annual expenses. An insurance company generally invests in Treasury bonds, so how could it possibly make 10 percent at a time such as 2016, with bonds yielding about 2 percent?

There's only one way: the company takes your money, "guarantees" that string of payments, and waits for you to die, hoping some of your money will still remain for it to keep. The actuaries know how to play the odds so that the company makes money. As for you,

you are spinning a roulette wheel. If you live to be ninety-five or one hundred, you win. If you die soon after annuitizing the contract, you lose. Your family loses in any case because the house keeps your money when you die.

The salespeople will be long gone. Nobody will be helping you over time with the investments of that portfolio. It will be operating on a wing and a prayer and the financial strength of the insurance company, which can be an issue for you since some of the huckster types use lower-rated companies that offer them higher commissions. When the time comes that you decide to start your payments, they will be based on the market value of that portfolio, which will not necessarily produce 6 percent a year. The only way to get a "guaranteed" rate moving forward is to annuitize the contract. You will be required to sign a waiver of understanding in which you agree that when you die (or when your spouse dies, if it's a joint situation), the insurance company will keep whatever principal remains.

From the insurance company's perspective, that's quite a deal. Registered investment advisors and even brokers cannot use that G word of "guarantee" when selling investment products. Only the insurance companies can offer that, and that's because they keep your money and have a strong lobby in Washington that allows them to keep that advantage over securities companies.

For some people, annuities can be a good idea, especially for single people without children who really don't care about where their money goes. They give the insurance company their money, and they get a payment every month for the rest of their life. Annuities may also be beneficial for certain "special-needs" trust situations where there are limited family members to assist with the needs of a disabled person.

So annuities do have limited use, but they are not being marketed that way. They are marketed to couples with families, and as soon as the unsuspected hear the G word, the brain stops working. A 6 percent guarantee gets ingrained in the brain, and nothing else registers.

People hear what they want to hear. "Yes, Virginia, there is a Santa Claus" and "Yes, there is a free lunch"—but the fact is, there are no free lunches in finance. The old adage, knowledge is power, applies here.

POWER IN YOUR PORTFOLIO

Again, the number-one rule, as you plan for that positive cash flow in retirement, is this: don't give your money away.

That of course raises the question of what you do instead, and it comes down to wisely investing your savings. How do you do that? Most people would respond, "Well, you diversify your assets"—and of course that is true, although it's not that simple. If you overdiversify, you can miss out on good equity markets, and that's really where you will be getting your additional principal (growth) during retirement. Even in a climate where equities only earn 6 percent (historical average) a year rather than the 8 or 10 percent we have seen in the past, for most people, that is better than getting 2 percent from a bond.

With the bond market showing instability since 2014, a standard sixty-forty portfolio mix of 60 percent equities and 40 percent bonds may not be reliable to provide income over time as it has in the past. This is where you need good financial advice. Not only are there different types of bonds, but someone needs to be watching all parts of the portfolio, not just the equities.

If you overdiversify, you run the risk of what investment managers sometimes call "de-worsification." You can get to the point where you have so many elements in a portfolio that most of them are not working. Traditionally, diversification has meant assets are placed in the four major asset classes: stocks, bonds, commodities, and commercial real estate investment trusts (REITs). That is a strategy that has worked over time and will continue to work over time. The question is: How much time do you have?

In 2015, for example, three of those four asset classes—bonds, commodities, and to some extent real estate—did not do well. In such a case, you wouldn't be happy with a perfectly balanced portfolio of the four major asset classes. It also wasn't a great year for US equities. What did work were certain sectors of the US economy. As you can see, it gets complex. In 2015, you would have been better off not diversifying so much and actually having a more concentrated portfolio. However, concentration brings risk; if you get it wrong, you can lose even more money. This is not just about market risk. This involves sector risk as well.

A competent advisor can help you sort this all out. Advisors cannot prevent you from losing money in a year as bad as 2008, but they can certainly limit the downside risk. Good advisors should be able to tell you the extent of your downside risk. They should be able to identify what is known as "upside capture" and "downside capture."

What does that mean? Well, most people realize that the S&P 500 and the Dow Jones indexes are broad measures of the US stock market. Investors measure the performance of their portfolios against how well those indexes are doing. Most people also know that if you want to hold down risk, you cannot put all of your money into the stock market. Investors therefore diversify into other asset classes and sectors that might not lose the same way as the S&P or the Dow. That's true diversification, but it is complex and calls for professional guidance *(see fig. 8.1; diversification of a "stock only" portfolio).*

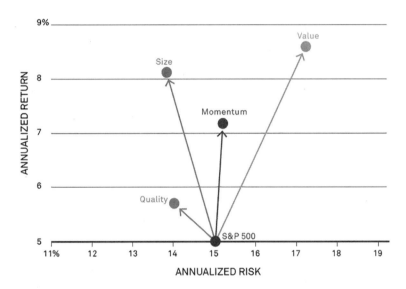

"MOVING NORTH" SEEKING OUTPERFORMANCE – US FACTORS
January 2001 - December 2015

Source: MSCI as of December 31, 2015. Index returns are for illustrative purposes. Index performance returns do not reflect management fees, transactions costs or expenses. Indexes are unmanaged and one cannot invest directly in an index. This analysis contains back-tested index data. For additional information, see Appendix. Momentum is represented by the MSCI USA Momentum Index. Quality is represented by the MSCI USA Sector Neutral Quality Index. Value is represented by the MSCI USA Value Index. Size is represented by the MSCI USA Risk Weighted Index.

BlackRock, Andrew Ang, PhD

Fig. 8.1

The Darwinian perspective is that those who survive over time are those who can best adapt to their environment. Adaptive investing is the key to maintaining a reasonable return over your lifetime. Yes, that is easier said than done, but it is nonetheless fundamental. If an advisor cannot tell you the meaning of "upside capture" and "downside capture," then you need to talk to someone else because that is the key to investing. These terms do not imply guarantees, just guidelines to expected price movement over time—an understanding of how portfolio values can fluctuate in different market environments.

If the S&P 500 is up 1 percent in a week or month, a portfolio that is designed with lesser risk than the S&P might be up only 0.8 percent for that day. If over the course of a year the Dow is up 10 percent, a less-risky portfolio might only make 8 percent. That is an 80 percent upside capture. A more conservative portfolio might make 7 percent, and a really conservative one might make only 5 percent— in other words, upside captures of 70 percent and 50 percent.

If that reflects your risk level, then you might be content with those limited upside captures. That's where you want to be. You don't require more than that, because you don't want the risk. You don't want to witness the higher volatility and the prospect of experiencing what happened to many portfolios in 2002 and 2008.

And what if the economy did experience a year such as 2008, when the broad averages dropped almost 40 percent? Portfolios designed like the S&P and the Dow were down 40 percent, and ones that were heavy in commercial real estate were down 60 percent. What if we had another experience like 2000–2002, when people were losing 80 percent of their money in tech stocks? Those were staggering losses.

Portfolios designed for downside capture, however, lost less. When the S&P was down 40 percent, a portfolio with the downside capture of 50 percent lost only half that much—in other words, it was down only 20 percent. Other strategies were down only 10 percent or even less. The only way to get the downside capture to zero is to buy into a hedge fund or managed futures account or fund. Most people should avoid those unless they get help from a competent advisor who understands the complexity of these styles.

An advisor who understands the issues can reduce the downside risk by adding certain features, with proper diversification, to a portfolio. For example, he or she might recommend that a small portion of money be placed in a managed-futures fund, a long/ short equity fund, or an exchange-traded fund with low or no correlation to the broad equity markets. These are products for professional management and guidance. Hedge funds work best in periods of high market volatility. For the average person who is investing through a rearview mirror, looking only at performance charts, they can become dangerous tools that can wreck a portfolio.

Good advisors will always be forward-looking at investing. They could be even a little early, but they really should understand inter-market relationships. In other words, if interest rates will be rising, as it appears will be happening in the next few years, certain investments should get less weight in a portfolio or be eliminated. Certain types of bonds can be underweighted. Certain types of bonds should be eliminated. Real estate might struggle in that environment. I say "might" struggle because the marketplace involves hundreds of variables, so you can never make definitive predictions. There is no easy black box in which we can know with certainty. That is why autopilot investing with low cost Internet custodians can be dangerous.

What we do know is that adaptive investing, with somebody monitoring the portfolio, brings the best results. In the years ahead, the rearview-mirror investors who use the online trading platforms, perhaps counting the stars on Morningstar, are likely to suffer losses. By contrast, professional advisors put asset classes and sectors on what we call a "heat map" *(see fig. 8.2)*. The ones that are on the top one year quite often are on the bottom the next year. In 1999, for

Source: SEI—Destination: Diversification. **This material has been obtained from sources generally considered reliable.** No guarantee can be made as to its accuracy. Not intended to represent the performance of any particular investment. Indices are unmanaged and one cannot invest directly in an index.

BEST → WORST (top to bottom)

2005	2006	2007	2008	2009	2010	2011	2012	2013	2014	2015
Emerging Markets Equity 34.54%	REIT Index 35.97%	Emerging Markets Equity 39.78%	International Fixed Income 8.01%	Emerging Markets Equity 79.02%	Small Cap Growth 29.09%	REIT Index 9.37%	Emerging Markets Equity 18.63%	Small Cap Growth 43.30%	REIT Index 32.00%	Large Cap Growth 5.67%
International Equity 14.02%	Emerging Markets Equity 32.59%	Large Cap Growth 11.81%	Core Fixed Income 5.24%	High Yield Bond 58.10%	REIT Index 28.07%	Emerging Market Debt 8.46%	Emerging Market Debt 18.54%	Small Cap Value 34.52%	Large Cap Value 13.45%	REIT Index 4.48%
REIT Index 13.82%	International Equity 26.86%	International Equity 11.63%	Emerging Market Debt -10.91%	Large Cap Growth 37.21%	Small Cap Value 24.50%	Core Fixed Income 7.84%	Small Cap Value 18.05%	Large Cap Growth 33.48%	Large Cap Core 13.24%	International Fixed Income 1.55%
Emerging Market Debt 10.73%	Small Cap Value 23.48%	60/40 Diversified Portfolio 7.98%	60/40 Diversified Portfolio -24.55%	Small Cap Growth 34.47%	Emerging Markets Equity 19.20%	High Yield Bond 4.37%	International Equity 17.90%	Large Cap Core 33.11%	Large Cap Growth 13.05%	Emerging Market Debt 1.23%
60/40 Diversified Portfolio 7.98%	Large Cap Value 22.25%	Small Cap Growth 7.05%	High Yield Bond -26.11%	International Equity 32.46%	Large Cap Growth 16.71%	International Fixed Income 4.06%	Large Cap Value 17.51%	Large Cap Value 32.53%	International Fixed Income 9.77%	Large Cap Core 0.92%
Large Cap Value 7.05%	Large Cap Core 15.46%	Core Fixed Income 6.96%	Small Cap Value -28.92%	REIT Index 28.46%	Large Cap Value 15.51%	Large Cap Growth 2.64%	REIT Index 17.12%	International Equity 23.29%	60/40 Diversified Portfolio 7.55%	Core Fixed Income 0.55%
Large Cap Core 6.27%	60/40 Diversified Portfolio 14.55%	Emerging Market Debt 6.28%	Large Cap Value -36.85%	Large Cap Core 28.43%	High Yield Bond 15.07%	Large Cap Core 1.50%	Large Cap Core 16.42%	60/40 Diversified Portfolio 16.52%	Core Fixed Income 5.97%	60/40 Diversified Portfolio -0.24%
International Fixed Income 5.69%	Small Cap Growth 13.35%	Large Cap Core 5.77%	Large Cap Core -37.60%	Emerging Market Debt 28.18%	Large Cap Core 15.06%	60/40 Diversified Portfolio 0.70%	High Yield Bond 15.55%	High Yield Bond 7.41%	Small Cap Growth 5.60%	International Equity -0.39%
Large Cap Growth 5.26%	High Yield Bond 10.76%	International Fixed Income 4.88%	Large Cap Growth -38.44%	60/40 Diversified Portfolio 26.28%	60/40 Diversified Portfolio 12.83%	Large Cap Value 0.39%	Large Cap Growth 15.26%	International Fixed Income 1.42%	Emerging Market Debt 5.53%	Small Cap Growth -1.38%
Small Cap Value 4.71%	Emerging Market Debt 9.88%	High Yield Bond 2.53%	Small Cap Growth -38.54%	Small Cap Value 20.58%	Emerging Market Debt 12.04%	Small Cap Growth -2.91%	Small Cap Growth 14.59%	REIT Index 1.22%	Small Cap Value 4.22%	Large Cap Value -3.83%
Small Cap Growth 4.15%	Large Cap Growth 9.07%	Large Cap Value -0.17%	REIT Index -39.20%	Large Cap Value 19.69%	International Equity 8.21%	Small Cap Value -5.50%	60/40 Diversified Portfolio 13.41%	Core Fixed Income -2.02%	High Yield Bond 2.51%	High Yield Bond -4.61%
High Yield Bond 2.78%	Core Fixed Income 4.33%	Small Cap Value -9.78%	International Equity -43.06%	Core Fixed Income 5.93%	Core Fixed Income 6.54%	International Equity -11.73%	International Fixed Income 5.51%	Emerging Markets Equity -2.27%	Emerging Markets Equity -1.82%	Small Cap Value -7.47%
Core Fixed Income 2.43%	International Fixed Income 3.10%	REIT Index -17.55%	Emerging Markets Equity -53.18%	International Fixed Income 2.38%	International Fixed Income 2.48%	Emerging Markets Equity -18.17%	Core Fixed Income 4.21%	Emerging Market Debt -6.58%	International Equity -4.48%	Emerging Markets Equity -14.6%

■ **60/40 Diversified Portfolio** = Annual returns for the 60/40 diversified portfolio are based on 24% Barclays Capital U.S. Aggregate Bond Index, 19% Russell® 1000 Growth, 18% Russell® 1000 Value, 12% MSCI EAFE, 6% MSCI Emerging Market, 6% Citigroup WGBI, Non-U.S., Hedged 4% Merrill Lynch U.S. High Yield Constrained, 4% J.P. Morgan EMBI Global, 3% Russell® 2000 Growth, 2% Russell® 2000 Value, and 2% Dow Jones DJ U.S. Select REIT Index.

The top-performing asset classes and sectors often are the worst performing positions the following year. Buy-and-hold strategies do not always work well.

Fig. 8.2

example, tech stocks were the best-performing asset class, while bonds were way down at the bottom of the scale. In 2000, tech stocks were at the bottom and bonds were near the top.

In the current environment, keeping your cash flowing in retirement will require serious research and monitoring. Rearview-mirror and autopilot investing are a setup for failure. It's unfortunate that people are retiring in this environment, but that's not something we can control. When you get to retirement age, the conditions are what they are.

You could just keep working, if that is an option, and we are seeing many baby boomers doing just that—that is, those whose occupations do not require heavy physical work. It's an interesting demographic. The United States no longer is a manufacturing economy. It is a service economy, and people with those kinds of jobs find that they are able to work longer. Working past your full retirement age can be a tremendous help to your cash flow because you are postponing the point where you start to withdraw income from your portfolio. Be careful, though: you could work yourself into an early grave doing that, but if you have the kind of job that won't wear you out, waiting a little longer to retire can be a good idea. If you are still interested (curious about new ideas) in your work, as many professionals say they are, keep going.

YOUR BEST ODDS FOR SUCCESS

According to research at the University of California, the people who are best at making predictions are not those you might think would be good at it. They are not the economists or finance people. They are not the doctors. In fact, of all the groups studied, the best at making predictions were the meteorologists. The weather people! Who'd have imagined?

Think about it, though. They use percentages to measure against the mean. They are never definitive in their prediction. "There's a 30 percent chance of rain," or "There's a 70 percent chance of snow." The use of percentages will get fairly close statistically to the predictive mean. They believe in what statistically is called "regression to the mean."

The lesson there is that when your portfolio is designed for percentages of upside and downside capture, your income and growth potential are more predictable. It's a matter of probability and statistics.

Another potentially useful approach is called the Monte Carlo simulation, which is a series of mathematical iterations on a probability. Using computer analysis, professionals might look at a thousand factors that could go into a portfolio mix and gauge the chances of success—whether that's 70, 80, or 90 percent, for example. This approach can be flawed because investing factors are influenced by too many events that are unpredictable in any given time, especially geopolitical and macroeconomic events. If this approach is used, the analysis should be redone annually.

But at least it is a measure. Professional guidance can significantly increase your chances of success. Let's face it, in a difficult year, portfolio values of even good advisors will decline. They certainly cannot walk on water, but they will be able to reduce the risk and the fear. Working with a proven process allows the investor to stay in the game without emotion until opportunity shows itself.

It is a creed among many doctors that they should first, if possible, cure the illness, and if this is not possible, to at least relieve the pain, and lastly, if no cure can be applied, to hold the patient's hand. That could be a principle among financial advisors, as well.

In a bad period, such as 2008, they did their best to relieve the pain and hold the hands, even as they strove for the cure. Just keeping the losses down to 10 percent instead of 40 percent was a great victory. You can easily make up a 10 percent loss; you just need to follow it with an 11 percent gain, as became available in 2009. But what about a 50 percent loss? As I explained earlier, that requires a gain of 100 percent to get back to even.

Once again, it comes down to positive cash flow, to having more coming in than is going out. That requires adapting throughout retirement to a rapidly changing environment, both socially and economically. Cash-flow analysis needs to be conducted annually, whether you do it on the back of the napkin or formally with a CFP® or the equivalent.

Just as you get an annual checkup with your doctor, it is wise to get one with a qualified financial advisor who can help you track the arc of your income and spending in your retirement years. This is critical. It's not just about the money. It's about knowing your direction and whether you are on the right track.

CHAPTER 9

PRESERVING YOUR ESTATE

Not all that long ago, estate planning was mostly about tax management. Early in my career, most of the estate planning in which I was involved had to do with preserving families' holdings by avoiding or eliminating those estate taxes.

In those days, the federal and state governments only granted a very limited amount of credit on an estate upon death. They heavily taxed the remainder of the family inheritance. Within the last twenty years, the amount of an estate that was exempted from taxes was at one point only $250,000. More recently, in 2001, it was $675,000. In other words, you would pay a tax of 50 percent on the value of your estate exceeding $675,000. Nobody wanted to see their children lose half of their inheritance, and so estate planning was quite a serious business.

I have long contended that estate taxes are the ultimate "taxation without representation." It descends upon you after you are gone. The tax man swoops in, and you can't say anything about it. Some people maintain that estate taxes amount to unconstitutional confiscation, and the question of whether they should be eliminated has been debated regularly in Congress.

All our lives, the opponents say, we get hit with taxes—state and federal income taxes, sales taxes, capital-gains taxes, and more—and then when we die, the government hungers for more. We are taxed to death, and then we are taxed *at* death. It's a big discussion, but don't expect that it will be settled anytime soon. With such a huge national debt, it would seem unlikely that the government will be getting rid of estate taxes anytime soon.

However, in recent years the rules have been changed for the better. The 2015 federal exemption from estate taxes was $5.43 million per person, meaning that a couple could have an estate of nearly $11 million before federal estate taxes would become an issue. Only the value above that amount is taxed at the federal level, although the inheritance tax of some states still kicks in at a lower threshold. Thirteen states still offer an exemption of only $675,000. The others have followed the federal exemption.

Why does this matter? Families with substantial assets certainly understand the toll this tax can take. The raising of the exemption has helped, but even now the value of an estate in many families easily can reach above $10.86 million, and when it does, the heirs lose half of any amount above that.

LIQUIDITY ISSUES

What complicates the situation for those families is that many of those assets often are illiquid, meaning they cannot be cashed in quickly. Money is tied up in a business, for example, or in real estate holdings. Upon death, all the holdings are considered part of the estate for taxation purposes. That includes the value of life insurance, unless it is in a life insurance trust that would place it outside of the estate. The estate includes the value of real estate, IRA accounts, pension plans, and more.

To raise money to pay the federal estate taxes, the family often has no choice but to sell some of those assets. Many years ago, for example, the family of Joe Robbie had to sell a substantial part of their interest in the Miami Dolphins ownership to pay the estate taxes. A football team certainly is marketable, so in that instance the family fared well. Not so in many other cases. It can be hard to sell real estate or a business quickly, and the government expects this to be done within a two-year window. When you are selling a property or a business under such circumstances, the buyers tend to know what's going on. It's like a fire sale, and you're not going to get top dollar. Not only that, but the overall real estate market may be dismal.

The raising of the estate-tax exemption to a much higher level has meant that taxes no longer are the huge issue as families plan how they will pass on a legacy. However, the issue of illiquid assets still needs to be managed carefully. Wealthy families with very large estates generally—though certainly not always—already will have the right advisors in place and have set up the trusts and other provisions to help protect their holdings. They need a qualified insurance agent, an accountant, and an attorney working together on those issues. They need a financial advisor as quarterback to identify and execute the right plays.

Collectibles, for example, can become a major estate problem for high-net-worth clients. Collectibles are wonderful things. As a child I collected bottle caps, for some reason, until one day my father asked me, "So what's with all these bottle caps?" At the time I thought it was cool but eventually understood they had little value and got rid of them.

A collector of Hummel figurines, however, is not saving bottle caps, and valuables such as that can present an estate issue. How do you get rid of a Hummel? An antique armoire might bring joy to the owner, but what if nobody really wants to inherit it? It will end up going to a dealer for a quarter on the dollar. A dealer likewise could get your coins and stamps for a bargain. I've seen it happen: a collector leaves $100,000 worth of stamps, and the family doesn't know what to do with them. It can happen with artwork, too. You might get fair value for a famous work if it is properly appraised and documented—but most people don't have Picassos around the house.

Not only are collectibles illiquid, but they can easily be stolen. Perhaps your father saw a TV ad and bought a collection of gold Krugerrands, which were shipped along with a cheap safe to store them in. Any thief could put that safe under an arm and walk out of the house. There's no reason to buy hard gold unless you think we're on the eve of Armageddon and want to take it with you to your underground bunker.

In the neighborhood in West Philadelphia where I was raised, an old man made a request to his wife that, upon his death, he wanted to be buried with his favorite pillow. Upon his demise his wife acquiesced to his request. Shortly after, at her bank, the widow was complaining to the teller about her financial demise. The teller asked her what happened to the $10,000 her husband took out of the account shortly before his death? After the bell went off in her head (can't imagine it took very long) she had the body exhumed and found the $10,000 tucked in the pillow under his head. I recall seeing new siding on her house shortly afterward.

Entire books have been written about the various elements of effective estate planning, and those are only a few of the considerations as families deal with the details upon the passing of their loved ones. There are many strategies by which wealthy people can get money out of their estate to protect it from taxes or to divert it to charity. Regardless of your ultimate estate intentions, an estate map should be charted to help visualize the many moving parts *(see fig. 9.1)*. Let's take a look at some of the overall issues and primary documents.

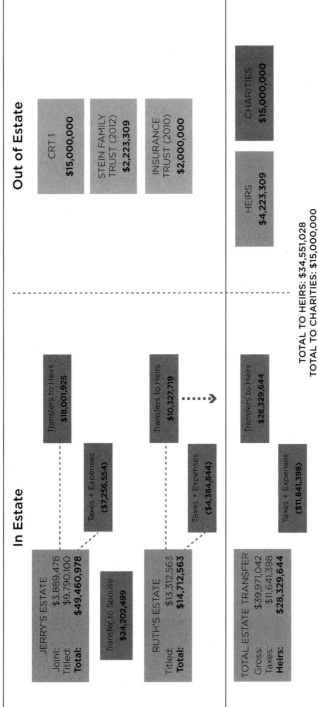

Estate Flow Chart
Base Facts as of November 2, 2015
Prepared for Mr. & Mrs. Sample

In Estate

JERRY'S ESTATE
Joint: $3,889,478
Titled: $9,790,100
Total: $49,460,978

Transfer to Spouse
$24,202,499

Transfers to Heirs
$18,001,925

Taxes + Expenses
($7,256,554)

RUTH'S ESTATE
Titled: $13,312,563
Total: $14,712,563

Transfers to Heirs
$10,327,719

Taxes + Expenses
($4,384,844)

TOTAL ESTATE TRANSFER
Gross: $39,971,042
Taxes: $11,641,398
Heirs: $28,329,644

Transfers to Heirs
$28,329,644

Out of Estate

CRT 1
$15,000,000

STEIN FAMILY TRUST (2012)
$2,223,309

INSURANCE TRUST (2010)
$2,000,000

CHARITIES
$15,000,000

HEIRS
$4,223,309

TOTAL TO HEIRS: $34,551,028
TOTAL TO CHARITIES: $15,000,000

Fig. 9.1

This analysis must be reviewed with the limitations and conditions disclosed in the Disclaimer page. Projections are based on assumptions provided by the advisor/representative, and are not guaranteed. Actual results will vary, perhaps to a significant degree. The projected reports are hypothetical in nature and for illustrative purposes only. Return assumptions do not reflect the deduction of any commissions. They will reflect any fees or product charges when entered by the advisor/representative. Deduction of such charges would result in a lower rate of return. Consult your legal and/or tax advisor before implementing any tax or legal strategies. © eMoney Advisory, LLC Reproduced with the permission of the copyright owner. Further reproduction prohibited without permission.

WILLS, TRUSTS, AND MORE

In its essence, estate planning is simply about disposition of assets. In other words, where do you want your resources to go? To family members? To the causes and institutions that you care about? Sorting it out requires professional assistance, not just to save on taxes but to help ensure that the right decisions are made in the best interest of posterity.

Dealing with these financial and family issues can take months of work and the coordinated efforts of professionals. Much is involved in managing the overall interests of a complicated estate, although some of the documents are fairly straightforward. You need to set up powers of attorney, for example, to have someone help manage your affairs or to assist your advisor if you become incapacitated at some point in your life. Another important document is a health-care directive, also known as a living will. If you become incapacitated to the point where you can no longer make your own decisions on end-of-life issues, such as whether you would want to be resuscitated or placed on life support, your health-care directive will designate someone with the authority to act in your stead who is fully aware of your wishes.

A basic document of estate planning is a will. Everyone needs one. It sounds almost too obvious to point out, but many people do not have one. It's not that a will is expensive. It's that they haven't bothered to take that step. They need to attend to that, and more, particularly if they have a high net worth. A simple will that distributes possessions—often called an "I love you" will—is insufficient.

People of high net worth need a more complex arrangement that may include various trusts. For example, a trust may be needed if a child or grandchild has special needs. The combination of a complex will and trust will direct the disposition of assets to precisely where they will serve best.

One of the functions of a trust, besides its potential to keep assets separate from the estate to protect it from taxation, is that it also can offer protection from lawsuits, creditors, and divorce claims. It is a natural desire that you would want the money that represents your life's work to stay in your family, and a trust that is carefully worded and properly set up can prevent it from being divvied up in a divorce. A trust can also shield that money from people who make false claims for money or who say they slipped on your sidewalk.

You might think of it this way: a trust gives you the ability to maintain control of your assets from the grave. In setting it up, you will be sitting down with your financial advisor and attorney to determine how you want the trust to be worded and managed. The trust can direct the disposition of your assets to your specifications, presuming they are within reason. For example, it would not be unreasonable to leave a child $10 million but insist that the trust distribute to her only a limited amount annually until a certain age is attained. Your attorney will help you with the rules and with the provisions, such as the ability to use the money for a beneficiary's "health, education, maintenance, and support," which are important legal terms. You can add other provisions, as well, and change them over time. This is not a fixed document. It is flexible and adaptable—until you die, of course, when it becomes irrevocable.

You also need to designate a trustee, someone reliable who you are confident will do right by your estate. That might well be someone in your family, but if you are concerned that a person lacks a good head for finances, you can get a corporate trustee, such as a bank or well-known securities custodian. A corporate trustee will charge a fee, usually reasonable, and then have the money invested with competent advisors.

If you want an advisory firm to handle the money, you can specify that in your will, and you can specify the custodian who will work with those advisors, perhaps the current custodian of your investment accounts. The trustee and the trust custodian will not be advising. They will do the administrative work; your advisory team can still manage the assets.

CHARITABLE TAX STRATEGIES

If you have charitable intentions, as a lot of people do, a charitable-remainder trust is a way to donate assets while retaining the income that they generate for as long as you live. Let's say you have $1 million that you would like to give to the cancer society, but you hesitate to do so because you need the income, perhaps $40,000 a year, from the investment of that money. If you put the money in a charitable-remainder trust, you can designate the cancer society as remainder beneficiary while still controlling the investment and collecting the return. You also get an immediate tax deduction for your donation; the charity can sell the assets free of taxes by virtue of its exempt status. Upon your death, the income stops, and the charity retains the remainder principal.

That is only one option for charitable giving. You and your estate attorney can discuss the potential tax advantages of donating stock or property that has a low-cost basis (price when the security was purchased). However, under current rules, if you leave low-basis property directly to your heirs, at your demise, they will get a step-up in basis for taxable assets they receive, whether that's stock or real estate or collectibles or anything else that has appreciated in value since the original purchase.

For example, you might have sizable holdings in a company that you bought at $2 a share in 1950. If you sold that stock now at $150 a share, you would owe a lot in taxes in the form of capital gains. After your death, however, your heir would receive it at the current value and owe no capital-gains tax. That means it might be a good idea to hold on to low-basis assets, unless it is likely that the asset will be plunging in value before you pass away. It seems that every year we see attempts to change that step-up rule so that the government can collect more tax, but as it stands, it is a tremendous estate-planning advantage that your advisor should understand.

If you are facing a serious estate-tax issue, giving assets away can be a good idea. Be careful, however: doing so can also be disastrous to your financial health. Quite often, people give away assets prematurely, and then, as they live to an old age, find that they should have kept that money because they need the income, perhaps to pay for extended care.

BEYOND YOUR LIFETIME

Effective estate planning requires projections far into the future, not only for the money you will need during your lifetime but also for what you hope to leave beyond your lifetime. Someone should be watching the cash flow all the way through your nineties, factoring in the financial issues. You need to be careful about emotions. It's nice to help your children, for example, but before you do so, you must be sure that you are not shortchanging yourself. What might seem like a great idea when you are relatively young and healthy could be cause for great regret later in life.

Many volumes have been written on estate planning, and the discussion can go on and on. There are generation-skipping trusts and dynasty trusts for passing on money efficiently to future generations. Those get complex, but estate-planning attorneys understand the rules and regulations. If you are highly affluent, there's only so much money that you can give to your children. With the proper estate-planning tools, you can continue to save on taxes by skipping to the next generation and giving money directly to the grandkids.

Affluent families have many options and strategies for efficiently passing on a legacy, but for most families—that is, those with estates smaller than the current exemption of nearly $11 million—estate taxes do not loom as large as they once did. But as the "millionaires next door" continue to multiply in number and in wealth, they will be requiring more complex estate planning. These issues must not be ignored. I have a client who waited two years to see an attorney to execute the changes we recommended for his complex estate. Fortunately, the procrastination didn't hurt his estate planning, and his situation ended well.

CONCLUSION

THE BEST IS YET TO BE

Financial independence is within reach of all, but how do you get there? How do you maintain your lifestyle in retirement after the paychecks stop? Answering those questions is what sound financial planning is all about. Not just anyone will do to help you along the way. A good financial advisor is one who has the knowledge and experience to recognize your issues and recommend the best strategy. A portfolio on autopilot will not lead you through a secure retirement.

In Niccolò Machiavelli's sixteenth-century political treatise, *The Prince*, he asserted that a prince demonstrates his own wisdom by choosing wise advisors. Others consider the prince to be competent himself if he has selected quality ministers. Machiavelli described three kinds of intelligence: The first is the kind that reaches understanding on its own—and the second gets it through others. The first is excellent, and the second is good. In essence, he was saying that those who have not attained wisdom must at least recognize it in others. The third type of intelligence—that which does neither—is useless, according to Machiavelli, and should be avoided.

In today's age, as in Machiavelli's, we still need to seek out wise advisors. Someone has to keep watch. And the advice must be in your best interest, not in the advisor's best interest. You don't want to consort with salesmen. They are like the third type of advisor that Machiavelli described. They are to be avoided. As he understood, to be intelligent does not necessarily mean to be smart. Your advisor must be both. Credentials matter, but they are not enough.

A smart advisor helps you to understand your options and reach the best decisions with the highest probability of success— and that means getting you to where you wish to be, however you have defined it. Once equipped with knowledge and tools, you can choose what suits you best. If your time and circumstances allow, you can take a chance on what's behind the curtains. If not, you can take the money and run. Either way, it will be a smart choice, not an emotional one based on fear or on greed.

In this book, I have sought to bring you a different narrative on financial advice, one you may never before have heard. To prosper on your path into and through retirement, you need primarily to understand two people: yourself and your advisor. You need to know yourself. What are your dreams? Why are you here? What's it all about? And you need to know your advisor. Is this someone you can trust with those dreams? Does he or she have the credentials and the smarts and the ethics to take you where you want to go? Together, you can go far. When the chemistry between you is strong and enduring, you have your best chance of attaining that nirvana known as financial independence. You can feel certain that the best is yet to be.

That sales advice I heard long ago in that New York training room still rings in my ears: "Keep the cherries, throw away the pits!" I have long since redefined those words as an axiom for attaining true wealth. Along your journey, pursue only what serves you well, and don't bother with the rest. I hope that what I have shared in these pages has helped you to see the difference.